MW00909431

curriculum connections

Civil War

Weapons, Tactics, and Strategy

BROWN
BEAR
BOOKS

Published by Brown Bear Books Ltd

4877 N. Circulo Bujia
Tucson
AZ 85718
USA

First Floor
9–17 St. Albans Place
London N1 0NX
UK

© 2011 Brown Bear Books Ltd

ISBN: 978-1-936333-46-2

Managing Editor: Tim Cooke
Designer: Joan Curtis
Picture Researcher: Sophie Mortimer
Art Director: Jeni Child
Editorial Director: Lindsey Lowe

Library of Congress Cataloging-in-Publication Data

Weapons, tactics, and strategy / edited by Tim Cooke.
  p. cm. -- (Curriculum connections : Civil War)
 Includes index.
 Summary: "In an alphabetical almanac format, describes the weapons used, tactics invented, and strategies employed by both sides during the U.S. Civil War"--Provided by publisher.
 ISBN 978-1-936333-46-2 (library binding)
 1. United States--History--Civil War, 1861-1865--Encyclopedias, Juvenile. 2. Military art and science--United States--History--19th century--Encyclopedias, Juvenile. I. Cooke, Tim, 1961- II. Title. III. Series.

 E468.W395 2012
 973.7--dc22

                    2011005412

Picture Credits

Cover Image
Thinkstock: Photos.com

Library of Congress: 7, 8, 16, 18, 31, 33, 36, 38, 40, 48, 58, 65, 69, 79, 82, 86, 90; National Archives: 12, 20, 22; 43, 51, 54, 56, 74, 77, 84, 94, 97, 99; Peter Newark American Pictures: 26; Robert Hunt Library: 29, 62, 67.

Artwork © Brown Bear Books Ltd

Printed in the United States of America

Contents

Introduction

Civil War forms part of the Curriculum Connections series. Each of the six volumes of the set covers a particular aspect of the conflict: Home Front and the Economy; Behind the Fighting; Weapons, Tactics, and Strategy; Politics; Battles and Campaigns; and People.

About this set

Each volume in *Civil War* features illustrated chapters, providing in-depth information about each subject. The chapters are all listed in the contents pages of each book. Each volume can be studied to provide a comprehensive understanding of all aspects of the conflict. However, each chapter may also be studied independently.

Within each chapter there are two key aids to learning that are to be found in color sidebars located in the margins of each page:

Curriculum Context sidebars indicate to the reader that a subject has a particular relevance to certain key state and national history guidelines and curricula. They highlight essential information or suggest useful ways for students to consider a subject or to include it in their studies.

Glossary sidebars define key words within the text.

At the end of the book, a summary **Glossary** lists the key terms defined in the volume. There is also a list of further print and Web-based resources and a full volume index.

Fully captioned illustrations play an important role throughout the set, including photographs and explanatory maps.

About this book

Weapons, Tactics, and Strategy explores the ways in which changes in technology affected the way in which the war was fought. At the start of the war, generals largely employed traditional tactics involving cavalry charges and close-quarter fighting. By the conflict's end, the development of long-range rifles and entrenched defenses foreshadowed the slaughter in the trenches of World War I (1914–1918).

In weapons, rifles could fire farther and more accurately. The machine gun was developed during the war, but not widely used. Artillery became more powerful and included siege guns designed to lob shells over defensive walls. The submarine made its first appearance in conflict. New battleships, covered in iron armor, marked a revolution in naval warfare; wooden-hulled ships were instantly obsolete, sparking a ship-building race among the leading maritime nations that would continue until World War I.

In terms of strategy, control of railroads and rivers became essential for the rapid movement of troops and the supply of armies. The North set out to break the Confederacy in two by cutting off communications between east and west. It also aimed to strangle the Southern economy by blockading Confederate ports. Confederate commanders meanwhile sought ways to invade the North and threaten Washington, D.C.

Artillery

Two main types of artillery were used during the Civil War. Highly mobile field artillery supported the troops on the battlefield. More powerful heavy artillery was used from fixed positions to attack and defend fortifications and ports.

The Union and Confederate armies employed guns of several kinds as field or heavy artillery. Smoothbore muzzleloaded cannons were the most common, but there were rifled guns, breechloading guns, and mortars. Some guns were highly specialized, such as the Union's 12-pounder (5.4-kg) mountain gun, which was only 33 inches (84 cm) long and could be carried by mule.

The Napoleon

The most versatile and widely used artillery piece was the Model 1857 12-pounder Napoleon, named for the French Emperor Napoleon III. When the Civil War broke out, only five Napoleons were in use. U.S. arsenals were still stocked with old Model 1841 6-pounders, which the Confederates seized when they captured federal arsenals in 1861. The 6-pounder was their main field gun in the first year of the war, but it lacked the range and power of the Napoleon. By July 1862, the Tredegar Works in Richmond, Virginia, the main Confederate gun foundry, was casting the 12-pounder. The Napoleon was a muzzleloaded smoothbore with a bronze barrel 5 feet 6 inches (168 cm) long. It had a range of up to 1,600 yards (1,463 m) and could fire four types of shot. The Confederacy made more than 450 Napoleons, compared with 1,127 produced in the Union.

Ammunition types

Solid shot was used against large bodies of enemy troops at long range or to batter enemy fortifications. A traditional cast iron cannonball weighing 12 pounds

(5.4 kg), it was the most accurate type of ammunition. The shrapnel shell was used against troops in the open or in trenches. Its accuracy depended on a timed fuse that started when the gun went off. Another ammunition type, the explosive shell, also depended on a fuse. This projectile was filled with about 8 ounces (225 g) of black powder. It was designed to penetrate and blow up fortifications and buildings.

Canister shot was used against attacking infantry and cavalry at close ranges of 350 yards (320 m) or less. Canister was a large tin can filled with 27 pieces of 1-inch (2.5-cm) diameter iron shot. As the gun was fired, the can split apart, releasing the shot and turning the artillery piece into a kind of giant shotgun. At times of extreme danger, artillerymen sometimes loaded their guns with double or even triple rounds of canister.

The most common method of firing artillery in the Civil War was by using a lanyard (a special rope) to pull and ignite a friction primer inserted into the rear vent (hole) of the gun. The friction primer was a copper tube filled

Curriculum Context

Curricula might ask students to analyze the effect of different weapons on the battlefield.

Shot

Small spherical pellets that are packed into canisters or shells.

Union artillery waiting to be transported in May 1863, including solid shot (foreground), coehorns, and Parrott guns (background).

with gunpowder that ignited when the lanyard pulled out a serrated wire.

Field guns were organized into batteries. In the Union army batteries were made up of six guns, manned by about 150 men commanded by a captain. In the Confederate army, which had fewer guns, a battery was reduced to four guns after 1861. The guns of a battery were positioned 14 yards (12.8 m) apart.

Rifled artillery

Rifled artillery began to appear soon after the war began. Rifled guns had a spiraled groove cut into the inside of the barrel that gave them greater range and accuracy than smoothbores such as the Napoleon. They were made of iron because the rifling groove wore away too quickly on bronze barrels. Rifled guns were easily identified by the big reinforcing bands of iron fitted at the rear of the barrel to strengthen the breech. Two designs were mainly used in the Union army, the 3-inch (7.6-cm) Ordnance Rifle and the 10-pounder (4.5-kg) Parrott gun. Their success led the Confederates to start making copies by 1863, though the Southern guns were generally inferior in quality.

Like the smoothbore cannon, the rifled guns were muzzleloaded. Breechloading guns were at the leading edge of technology, and both armies imported some from Britain. Breechloaders were not used in large numbers, however, as muzzleloaders could fire just as rapidly.

Curriculum Context

The Union had the advantage of a far more developed iron industry than the South.

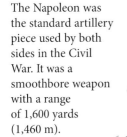

The Napoleon was the standard artillery piece used by both sides in the Civil War. It was a smoothbore weapon with a range of 1,600 yards (1,460 m).

Heavy artillery

The most powerful guns in the Civil War were those of the heavy artillery. They were made of iron, and by the end of the war most were rifled.

Moving and Firing Field Artillery

A six-horse team pulled the gun and the two-wheeled vehicle to which it was attached, known as a limber, while another team of six pulled the caisson, a wagon with extra ammunition, a spare wheel, and other accessories. Each team had three drivers; the rest of the crew either walked or sat on the limber and caisson. The pace was usually a steady trot when not under fire—galloping was only for emergencies. Field artillery was meant to be able to keep up with the cavalry, but its ability to do so depended on the condition of the roads, which often slowed down the batteries considerably.

The gun was brought into action by a commander and crew of six, who had to go through 14 maneuvers to load and fire. The drill was complicated, but an experienced team could arrive in position, unlimber, and fire their first shot in about 30 seconds. After that a fire rate of two shots a minute was a good average.

The heaviest guns a marching army could transport were siege guns, such as the 30-pounder (13.6-kg) Parrott gun. Bigger artillery pieces had to be mounted on a carriage (to control the massive recoil) and be installed within fortifications or entrenchments. Some of these guns were huge. The most powerful were the coastal artillery pieces used against shipping. The Union Rodman gun could fire a projectile weighing 1,080 pounds (490 kg) over 3 miles (5 km).

Mortars

The mortar was the other type of artillery used during the war. Mortars had a short, stubby barrel that could throw shells in a high arc at short range into fortifications. This made them ideal for sieges, and they were used in large numbers by the Union army. The largest mortars had a caliber of 13 inches (33 cm) and were sometimes mounted on railroad flatcars.

A much smaller bronze mortar, called the coehorn, was also used in sieges. It weighed about 290 pounds (131 kg) and could be carried by four men. The coehorn was used in the trenches around Petersburg, Virginia, in the fighting and siege of 1864 and 1865.

Recoil

The kickback of a gun or cannon as it is fired.

Curriculum Context

You could read more about the use of mortars in Union sieges such as those of Vicksburg, Petersburg, and Port Hudson.

Caliber

The diameter of a bullet or other projectile.

Black Troops

In the North politicians, soldiers, and abolitionists began to debate the question of whether or not black troops should be recruited by the Union army almost as soon as the war began in the spring of 1861.

Curriculum Context

Curricula might ask you to examine the motives of African American soldiers who fought in the Union armies.

The recruitment of black troops was controversial. People who supported the idea believed the Union should use all the men it could to win the war. They also saw an opportunity for black soldiers to win a more secure place in society for their race . Many of those who were against black recruitment echoed racist attitudes found in the South. As the whites debated, many free blacks tried to enlist. At this early stage in the war, however, the Lincoln administration was unwilling to enlist black soldiers. The government still viewed the conflict as a white-only struggle for the unity of the country rather than a war to end slavery.

The Union's changing policy

Two new laws of July 1862 reflected a shift in government attitudes. The Confiscation Act and Militia Act officially brought black people into the Union war effort and opened the way for the formation of black units in the army. The Confiscation Act stated that all escaped slaves who came under Union control would be free, and could be employed by the Union to suppress the Confederate rebellion. The Militia Act gave the president the power to enroll "persons of African descent" for "any war service," including as soldiers. Within weeks black regiments under white officers were being raised throughout the Union and in the Southern territories it controlled.

Militia

A military unit that is called upon only in times of emergency.

In New Orleans, Louisiana, the occupying Union governor, Benjamin Butler, raised three regiments of black militia, enlisting both freedmen and escaped slaves. On the South Carolina coast former slaves formed the 1st South Carolina Volunteer Regiment, while in the North freedmen joined the 54th Massachusetts. In the west the 1st Kansas Colored Volunteer Regiment was made up of ex-slaves from Arkansas and Missouri. This unit fought the first engagement by a black unit against the Confederates, at Island Mound, Missouri, in October 1862.

Although Union enlistment of black troops was underway by the end of 1862, discrimination was still widespread. Doubts were raised whether African Americans could fight, and many Union commanders saw black units merely as a source of labor to do menial or manual tasks. It was only in summer 1863 that black soldiers had the chance to prove their worth. On July 18 the 54th Massachusetts charged the Confederate stronghold at Fort Wagner, South Carolina. Although the assault failed, the regiment's courage proved the fighting quality of black soldiers.

Curriculum Context

Learn more about the 54th Massachusetts by watching the 1989 movie *Glory*, which tells their story.

Unequal pay

Black soldiers were not paid the same as white soldiers. A white Union soldier received on average $13 a month, plus a $3.50 clothing allowance; a black soldier only $10 a month less a $3 clothing deduction. Black soldiers received no financial bounty on enlistment as white volunteers did. Equal pay became a serious point of dispute with the Lincoln administration. Abolitionists campaigned for it. Men of the 54th Massachusetts Regiment, having been promised equal pay on their enlistment, refused any pay until the injustice was ended. It was only in June 1864 that Congress finally gave black troops equal pay.

Bounty

A one-off payment made to encourage men to enlist in the army.

Remember Fort Pillow

The Southern reaction to Union enlistment of black troops was violently hostile. The Confederates did not regard black soldiers as prisoners of war but treated

The Union began to recruit black troops at the end of 1862. This photograph shows men of the 4th U.S. Colored Infantry at Fort Lincoln—part of the Washington defenses.

them as runaway slaves. Jefferson Davis declared that their white officers would be treated as criminals. Black prisoners were often executed and many were sold back into slavery. Atrocities occurred, most notably at Fort Pillow, Tennessee, in April 1864, where only 62 of 262 black troops survived during the Confederate attack on a Union-held fort. "Remember Fort Pillow" became a rallying cry among black troops.

United States Colored Troops

In April 1863 Lorenzo Thomas, the adjutant general, traveled west to the Mississippi Valley to recruit regiments from the huge numbers of former slaves now living in areas under Union control. These new regiments eventually came under the control of the Bureau of Colored Troops in Washington and were designated United States Colored Troops (USCT). Thomas met with tremendous success. By the end of 1863, he had raised 20 regiments; a year later he had 50. More than 180,000 men served in USCT infantry, cavalry, and artillery regiments during the war, the majority from the states of Kentucky, Louisiana, Tennessee, and Mississippi. By the end of the Civil War black troops made up 10 percent of the Union army, although only about 100 out of the tens of thousands recruited were commissioned as officers. Sixteen black soldiers received the Medal of Honor.

Union navy

The Union navy recruited black sailors from the start. Faced with a huge manpower shortage, it enlisted both free blacks and runaway slaves. Between 1861 and 1865 about 18,000 black sailors served in the navy, making up 15 percent of the total enlisted force. Although no black sailor was ever promoted to officer rank, eight black sailors received the Medal of Honor for bravery in battle.

Medal of Honor

The Medal of Honor for gallantry in action was created by President Lincoln in 1863.

Confederate attitudes

In the Confederate states it was a point of principle among many not to allow blacks to become soldiers but senior officers recognized the Confederacy's need for more soldiers, even if it meant freeing slaves.

In February 1865 Robert E. Lee urged President Jefferson Davis to recruit slaves, and by March 13 the Confederate Congress had passed a law authorizing the use of black troops. On April 1, 1865, Colonel Otey of the 11th Virginia Infantry was ordered to recruit and train black units for the Confederate army, but it was too late. The end of the war and the end of the Confederacy came within a month.

A Liberating Army

Letter from Private Spotswood Rice, a Missouri black soldier, to his enslaved daughters.

"September 3, 1864

"My children, I take my pen in hand to rite you a few lines to let you know that I have not forgot you and that I want to see you as bad as ever now my dear children. I want you to be contented with whatever may be your lots. Be assured that I will have you if it cost me my life on the 28th of the month. 8 hundred White and 8 hundred blacke solders expects to start up the rivore to Glasgow and above there thats to be [led] by a general that will give me both of you. When they come I expect to be with them and expect to get you both in return. Don't be uneasy my children. I expect to have you. If Diggs [Kitty Diggs; the slave-owner] don't give you up this Government will and ... I want her to remember if she meets me with ten thousand soldiers she will meet her enemy."

Cavalry

In 1860 there were only five regiments of cavalry in the U.S. Army. By the end of the war the Union had more than 170 cavalry regiments, while the Confederates had more than 130 cavalry regiments and 100 independent cavalry battalions.

The basic cavalry component on both sides was a regiment commanded by a colonel. A Confederate cavalry regiment was made up of some 10 companies of between 60 to 80 men. In the Union army a cavalry regiment had about 1,000 men divided into six squadrons, each containing two troops of up to 100 men. The organization was simplified in 1863, and the squadron was replaced by battalions of four troops.

Every cavalry regiment had a blacksmith and a farrier (who shoed the horses). A Union cavalry regiment also took along a surgeon, his assistant, and two hospital stewards—luxuries most Confederate outfits could not afford. The numbers in each unit varied widely on campaign, since most cavalry units, particularly on the Confederate side, were always understrength.

Horses
One of the great differences between the Union and Confederate cavalry was that Southern troopers had to supply their own horses. The system worked well in the first years of war, because the South was largely rural and most volunteers could supply their own mounts. As the war went on and losses of horses through battle, sickness, and sheer exhaustion took their toll, however, the numbers of Confederate cavalry dwindled as cavalrymen who had no horse to ride had to leave their companies to find new mounts. Attempts by the army to make these men fight on foot as infantry usually failed: most cavalrymen would sooner desert than become infantrymen.

Curriculum Context

The Union's economic superiority impacted the conflict in many ways.

Curriculum Context

Both cavalrymen and artillerymen saw themselves as superior to the ordinary infantryman.

The Union government also started the war asking volunteer regiments to supply their own horses to save money. Cavalry were the most expensive soldiers to equip: a single regiment might cost up to $600,000. By July 1863 the Union War Department had established the Cavalry Bureau to buy mounts for the cavalry. Within a year 150,000 horses had been purchased and supplied through two depots, one in Washington, D.C., and one in St. Louis, Missouri.

Cavalry weapons

The three basic cavalry weapons were the saber, the carbine, and the pistol. The 6th Pennsylvania Cavalry, a regiment known as Rush's Lancers, carried a 10-foot wooden lance but it was abandoned—unused—by 1863. The saber, with its 3-foot-long (90-cm) curved blade, was designed to be the Union's main offensive weapon. Many Confederate cavalrymen regarded it in the same way as the lance. They preferred large-caliber pistols such as the six-shot Colt Navy, although Union cavalry carried sabers throughout the conflict and found that they could still be effective in close combat.

The Union cavalry had the edge in firepower when it came to the carbine. There were various patterns of this short-barreled weapon. One of the most common

Lance
A long, metal-tipped spear carried by horsemen.

Saber
A heavy sword with one sharp edge and a slightly curved blade.

A Cavalryman's Belongings

In April 1861, as volunteers mustered for the first time, many carried more gear than they could cope with. A Confederate cavalryman recruited into the W.P. Rangers, a Texas cavalry company, remembered his baggage even before he received his official weapons and ammunition:

"Myself, saddle, bridle, saddle-blanket, curry comb, horse brush, coffee pot, tin cup, 20 lbs. of ham, 200 biscuits, 5 lbs. ground coffee, 5 lbs. sugar, one pound cake presented to me by Mrs. C. E. Talley, 6 shirts, 6 pairs socks, 3 pairs draws, 2 pairs pants, 2 jackets, 1 pair heavy mud boots, one Colt's revolver, one small dirk [dagger], four blankets, sixty feet of rope with a twelve inch iron pin attached ... and divers and sundry little mementoes from friends."

Carbine

A light, short-barreled, repeating firearm designed to be used by cavalry.

types used by the Union cavalry was the Sharps. The most advanced carbine was the Spencer breechloading repeater, which fired seven rounds before reloading. By 1865 the Union army had issued over 80,000 Sharps and 90,000 Spencers. The Confederates began the war with muzzleloaders and even shotguns. Later they used breechloaders mostly captured from Union forces.

Cavalry tactics

The breechloading carbine was one reason why cavalry tactics changed so much. In 1861 it was still believed a line of saber-wielding troopers could drive infantry off the battlefield in a single charge. The Confederate cavalry commander J.E.B. Stuart achieved this feat at the First Battle of Bull Run (Manassas) on July 21, 1861, though his success was more to do with the Union infantrymen's inexperience. Later in the war veteran infantry stood firm behind cover, relying on the range and power of their rifled muskets to stop a cavalry charge. In previous wars infantry stood little chance of surviving a charge of cavalry, but Civil War infantry with rifled muskets accurate up to 300 yards (275 m) could turn a cavalry attack into a suicide charge.

Curriculum Context

The decline of traditional cavalry charges was one of the major tactical changes of the Civil War; it influenced many future wars.

Cavalry raids

Denied their traditional role as shock-troops and battle-winners, by 1862 both cavalries were struggling to find a new contribution to make. The Union cavalry

Alfred Pleasonton (right) and George A. Custer, two of the Union's best cavalry commanders, in Falmouth, Virginia, April 1863.

Stuart's Ride Around McClellan

One of the most spectacular cavalry raids took place in June 1862, when J.E.B. Stuart, by then a brigadier general and Confederate General Robert E. Lee's cavalry chief, took 1,200 men on a daring three-day ride around Union General George B. McClellan's army encamped on the Virginia Peninsula outside Richmond.

Stuart awoke his cavalrymen at 2:00 a.m. on the first day of the ride and told them to be in the saddle in ten minutes. In all, the Confederates rode 100 miles (160 km) around the 100,000-strong Union army, taking prisoners, plundering supplies, and sabotaging railroad tracks. Stuart also brought back valuable information to Lee about the position of McClellan's army. During the entire raid he lost only one of his men and one piece of artillery.

The raid was hailed as a great success and an example of Southern dash and courage, boosting the Confederates' morale and further enhancing Stuart's reputation. One of Stuart's staff officers recalled, "Everywhere we were seen, we were greeted with enthusiasm. General Stuart's name was praised and celebrated in every manner."

was still a young and inexperienced force used mainly to guard supply lines and encampments. The Confederate cavalry, which had better leadership and finer horsemen, began to specialize in large-scale raids and reconnaissance operations, such as J.E.B. Stuart's ride around George B. McClellan's Union army (see box). As the war went on, cavalry units from both sides served behind the lines as guerrilla fighters.

Raids behind enemy lines, distracting and confusing the enemy, did wonders for the cavalry's reputation and raised morale. But while the cavalry was raiding, it could not concentrate on its other vital task of keeping a watch on the enemy's movements. This failure had serious consequences. At Chancellorsville in May 1863 Union General Joseph Hooker sent his cavalry on a raid and, as a result, was not warned of the arrival of Lee's army from Fredericksburg. Two months later, in Pennsylvania, Lee was let down by J.E.B. Stuart, who, in an attempt to repeat his exploit on the peninsula was not in a position to warn his commander that the Union army was concentrating at Gettysburg.

Reconnaissance

Something done for the purpose of gathering information about the enemy, their position, and plans.

Curriculum Context

Was it worth overlooking reconnaissance duties in order to boost public and military morale?

Union officers of
C and D companies,
1st Massachussetts
Cavalry, near
Petersburg, Virginia,
August 1864.

These failures were partly responsible for the cavalry's poor reputation among the infantry of both sides, who were doing most of the fighting and dying. "Whoever saw a dead cavalryman?" was a common infantry jibe.

New tactics

During 1863 the Confederate cavalry began to decline, through a lack of recruits, horses, and weapons. The Union cavalry meanwhile were growing stronger, and were taking a more offensive role by adopting tactics of mounted infantry. Their horses gave the troopers mobility on the battlefield, while the carbine, especially the Spencer, gave them the firepower to hold positions against Confederate infantry when fighting on foot.

Union cavalry at Gettysburg

Two brigades of John Buford's 1st U.S. Cavalry Division, fighting in this way, held off two Confederate divisions on the first day of the Battle of Gettysburg on July 1, 1863. From cover behind a stone wall the cavalrymen fought for two hours until reinforced by infantry, making sure that the Army of the Potomac held the high ground that proved decisive to the outcome of the battle. This was not cavalry warfare in the classic saber-charging European style, but it suited the Civil War soldier and the kinds of battle he fought. In later decades it helped change cavalry tactics around the world.

Curriculum Context

Gettysburg features in many curricula as one of the major turning points of the war.

Communications and Signals

The Civil War was a period of great improvement in military communications. While both sides still sent written messages by mounted courier, they also used a new visual signaling system and the electric telegraph.

The Civil War was fought over a vast area of hundreds of square miles by armies that numbered tens of thousands. For the armies to operate effectively, often in remote locations, they needed an efficient signaling system.

Wigwagging

Albert J. Myer, a doctor, who studied sign language for the deaf, put his knowledge to military use and in 1856 invented a method of signaling using flags in the daytime and lamps at night. Known as the wigwag system, the U.S. Army tried it out on the western frontier before the war. The system was based on two separate signal movements of either the flag or lamp, which stood for the numbers 1 and 2. Different combinations of these two signals identified letters, whole phrases, or numbers. A pause signaled the end of one letter and the beginning of the next. A third signal movement marked the end of each word.

Code-breaking

Both armies used the same signaling system at the beginning of the Civil War. This created serious problems because confidential messages from one side could be read by the other. The problem was only solved by sending messages in code (using words with secret meanings) or cipher (scrambled messages). This led to a code-breaking war as teams of cryptanalysts (code-breakers) on both sides worked to decipher the messages sent and received by the enemy. The Confederate Signal Bureau expanded this secret area of its work during the war and took responsibility for the Confederacy's spy networks, which were run by its secret service division.

Wigwagging messages was slow—three words per minute—but the signals could be sent 20 miles (32 km) on a clear day. The system proved its value time and again. At Allatoona, Georgia, in October 1864, the Union army used it to call in reinforcements. After the war broke out, Myer set up the Signal Camp of Instruction at Georgetown, Washington, D.C. Myer's work was only semiofficial, and the Union signal service remained disorganized until the federal government established the U.S. Army Signal Corps in August 1864.

Curriculum Context

What reasons might there be for taking so long to organize Union communications services?

U.S. Army Signal Corps

The Signal Corps consisted of 167 officers, 84 NCOs (noncommissioned officers), and 1,266 privates, all commanded by a colonel. Each army and corps headquarters in the field had a signal department. By 1865 the corps stood at 300 officers and 2,500 men.

Confederate Army Signal Bureau

The Confederates were the first to use Myer's system in battle. Captain Edward P. Alexander, a former assistant of Myer's, was on the staff of Pierre G.T. Beauregard's army at Manassas. He organized a series of signal posts. The system was operational for the first time at the First Battle of Bull Run on July 21, 1861. It gave the warning of a Union flanking march, saving the Confederates and paving the way for their victory later in the day.

Bull Run

The Confederate victory in the first battle of the Civil War shocked the Union public.

A Union signal tower on Elk Mountain, overlooking the battlefield of Antietam, Maryland, in September 1862. Signalmen had to send messages from a prominent and visible position, which made them vulnerable to enemy snipers.

Above the White House

The telegraph was used to send messages from one of the war's most interesting innovations, the hydrogen balloon. Thaddeus S.C. Lowe, an "aeronaut," traveled to Washington in June 1861 to sell to the War Department his idea for a Union Balloon Corps to observe Confederate troop positions from the air. Lowe linked his balloon Enterprise to the telegraph system and ascended 1,000 feet (305 m) above the White House. Lowe then sent President Lincoln a telegram from his excellent vantage point: "The city, with its girdle of encampments, presents a superb scene."

It was a brilliant piece of public relations. The government set up a Union Balloon Corps that year. Lowe received funding for seven new balloons, two of which, the *Constitution* and *Intrepid*, were used during George B. McClellan's Peninsular Campaign of 1862.

The Confederate Army Signal Bureau was established in April 1862. It was commanded by a major with 30 officers and 10 sergeants. It had no private soldiers; they were simply detailed from the line of the army when they were needed. Each army division and cavalry brigade was assigned its own signal squad of five privates commanded by a sergeant or lieutenant.

Signaling equipment
The wigwag signal flags were large and designed to be clearly visible by powerful telescopes over long distances. The most common types were a white flag with a red square in the middle (for use at twilight) and a red flag with a white square (for broad daylight). In winter signalmen used black flags because they showed up against the snow.

Signal posts
To transmit a message along an army's battle line, which could extend up to 6 miles (10 km), a series of signal posts was set up within sight of one another. An officer or NCO read off the message and an enlisted man worked the flag or lamp. These posts were often on high ground or even in tall trees. During the Siege of Petersburg, Virginia, in 1864–1865 Union troops

NCO
Non-commissioned officer: a junior officer who has been promoted from the ranks of the army.

occupied their trench lines for so long that the army built a series of wooden signal towers, some of which were up to 140 feet (43 m) tall. A signalman's work could be very dangerous. He was a prime target for sharpshooters and artillery batteries hoping to disrupt the enemy's communications.

The electric telegraph

The telegraph, first developed in the 1840s, was another important method of communication. By 1861 the United States had 50,000 miles (80,000 km) of telegraph wire crisscrossing the country, providing the fastest method of communication yet achieved. The Union government recognized the telegraph could be a war-winning technology and acted swiftly to gain control of it. In April 1861 the Union government seized all the commercial telegraph systems around Washington, D.C., and in early 1862 the War Department took over all private lines and railroad telegraphs. To run the system, the Military Telegraph Corps was set up in November 1861. It was a separate organization from the Signal Corps and was run directly from the War Department in Washington. Army commanders had no control over it, which caused some friction between the telegraphers and Signal Corps officers. The job the telegraphers did, however, was vital in waging war on a continental scale. By 1865 they had established over 15,000 miles (24,000 km) of new lines and sent and received 750,000 messages a year.

The Confederates, who lacked the resources of the Union, did not have a separate telegraph corps. Instead, the Signal Bureau worked with privately owned telegraph companies to provide the army with a basic system. The Confederates also used the Union's telegraph system for their own benefit. Partisan cavalry working behind the lines became skilled at tapping into the system to read messages or to send false information to Union commanders.

A soldier from the Union Corps of Engineers repairs a telegraph wire. The telegraph allowed generals in the field to communicate quickly with the government in Washington.

Confederate Army

The Confederacy began to organize its armies barely a month before the Civil War broke out in April 1861. The regular army was soon dwarfed by the provisional Confederate army, made up of 12-month militiamen and volunteers.

The Confederacy started the war with very little in the way of armed forces. State militias were organized by and remained within their home state. As each state seceded and declared itself an independent entity, its own army might emerge.

The prewar South had a strong military tradition, with three military colleges—the Virginia Military Institute, the Citadel in Charleston, South Carolina, and what later became Louisiana State University, as well as a great many other military schools. They gave the Confederacy a steady supply of junior officers for the lower levels of command. The North had only the U.S. Military Academy at West Point. West Point supplied most of the senior officers in the U.S. Army. When the war began, the Confederacy attracted the services of about the same number of U.S. Army officers and West Point graduates as did the Union.

Field forces

The term "army" applies not only to the entire Confederate force—the "Confederate army"—but also to individual field forces. There were at least 23 separate Confederate armies during the war, though not all at the same time. The main Confederate army was the Army of Northern Virginia, commanded for most of the war by Robert E. Lee. It served principally in the eastern theater (east of the Appalachian Mountains). The main army in the western theater (between the Appalachians and the Mississippi River) was the Army of Tennessee.

Militias

Local forces of civilian volunteers who could perform military duties in times of emergency.

Curriculum Context

Students might be asked to discuss the kinds of loyalties that made officers choose to stay with the Union or join the Confederacy.

Curriculum Context

Robert E. Lee's command of the Army of Northern Virginia is one of the most significant individual contributions to the war.

The first Confederate army was the Army of South Carolina. It was originally a state force made up of various militia units, volunteers, and cadets from the Citadel. President Jefferson Davis appointed Pierre G.T. Beauregard as the Confederacy's first brigadier general and sent him to Charleston. Beauregard took governmental control of the Army of South Carolina, which became the Confederates' first national force.

The Confederates typically named their armies for states or regions. Like the Union, the Confederacy divided its territory into military departments but they placed much more emphasis on the system, which proved to be ultimately unsatisfactory. A military department was a large administrative area of one or more states. Each department had a commander, who was in theory also the commander of any field army in his area. However, the system worked poorly because the responsibilities of the department commander were not clearly defined in relation to the commanders of the armies. As a result, troops were often not positioned near enemy units, and troops in any given department did not cooperate with each other.

Jefferson's errors
The Confederacy was fortunate to get its more able men into key positions at the start of the war. The advantage was lost, however, by President Jefferson

This diagram shows the typical structure of a Confederate army.

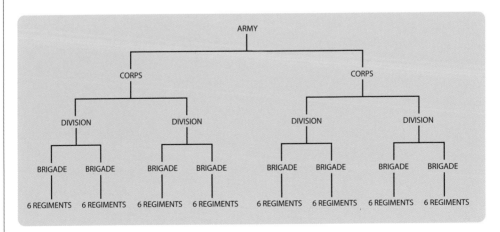

Ragged Confederates

Major General E. M. Law described the Confederate Army of Northern Virginia as it appeared in spring 1865:

"The army had ... never been so scantily supplied with food and clothing. The equipment as to arms was well enough for men who knew how to use them, but commissary and quartermasters' supplies were lamentably deficient. A new pair of shoes or an overcoat was a luxury and full rations would have astonished the stomachs of Lee's ragged Confederates. But they took their privations cheerfully and complaints were seldom heard.

"I have often heard expressions of surprise that these ragged, barefooted, half-starved men would fight at all. ... [That] they remained with their colors through such privations and hardships was sufficient to prove that they would be dangerous foes to encounter upon the line of battle. The morale of the army ... was excellent."

Davis, who made three key errors. He raised his classmate and friend, Leonidas Polk, to the rank of general. Polk never performed very satisfactorily. Despite this, he was allowed to stay in his post until his death in 1864. Davis also retained faith for too long in Braxton Bragg, who had impressed him early in the war, but who proved inadequate as a highly placed combat commander. Even when Davis finally removed Bragg from field command, he made him a principal military adviser. Last, Davis made a mistake in giving command of an army to John Bell Hood, who had been promoted beyond his competence.

Army organization

The largest component in the armies of both sides was the corps, a system adopted from the French army. There were typically two or three corps in a Confederate army, while a Union army had seven or eight smaller corps. Confederate units were often named for their commanders or former commanders, which was confusing when the commander was transferred. The Confederates placed regiments from the same state in the same brigades whenever possible, which raised morale and allowed brigades to

Corps
A military unit consisting of two or three divisions; the Union began using corps in March 1862, the Confederates in November 1862.

Confederate Private Thomas Taylor of the 8th Louisiana Infantry, in full kit, armed with a musket.

Curriculum Context

The great French general Napoleon Bonaparte once said that, in war, morale was to physical strength as three was to one.

develop a distinct identity. Famous examples include Hood's Texas brigade of Lee's Army of Northern Virginia and the 1st Kentucky (Orphan) brigade of the Army of Tennessee. Armies on both sides were organized around the infantry. Civil War battles, with few exceptions, principally involved infantry fighting with rifled muskets, supported by the cavalry and artillery. The Confederate cavalry was a great strength: It completely outclassed the Union cavalry, at least in the first two years of the war. But the Confederacy was at a disadvantage regarding weapons and ammunition, partly because it had fewer manufacturing facilities.

Quality of soldiers

More Southerners at the outset of the fighting were comfortable with outdoor life, just as they were better horsemen. But Northern soldiers gradually caught up. More important was the fact that many more Northern soldiers had some kind of occupational training, and far more had been exposed to typical childhood diseases. Huge numbers of Southerners succumbed to measles, including an entire garrison at Camp Moore, a Louisiana training facility.

Morale, religion, and thoughts of family back home were very important for the soldiers. Confederate morale was often good despite difficult conditions. Historians still debate how much the soldiers were motivated by commitment to a cause. Some consider ideology to have been very important, while others believe it had little effect. The regiment and brigade structure was certainly very significant—much of the soldiers' motivation came from their commitment to their comrades in arms. The Confederacy's lack of resources badly affected the army. Soldiers were often hampered by a lack of equipment, clothing—especially boots and shoes—and food. Despite such difficulties, the Southerners hung in doggedly for a remarkably long time.

Confederate Navy

At the outbreak of war the Confederate states had few ships or shipyards and little naval tradition. They tried to make up for this with resourcefulness and several innovations such as the sea mine (then called the torpedo.)

The Confederacy's first and only secretary of the navy, Stephen R. Mallory, had almost no vessels under his control when his Department of the Navy came into being in February 1861. There was only a single naval facility—confiscated from the U.S. Navy at Pensacola, Florida. Virginia's secession two months later brought the important Norfolk naval yard into Confederate hands, but only after evacuating Union forces had significantly damaged it. Of the 1,457 officers of the prewar U.S. Navy, only 237 cast their lot with the Confederacy. Outgunned by the Union navy, Mallory followed a traditional American naval strategy based on coastal defense, commerce raiding, and, later, blockade-running.

The ironclads

Unable to compete with the enemy on numerical terms, Mallory substituted innovation for quantity. The 1860s were a time of transition in naval technology. None of the world's navies had yet settled on a warship design that would make the best use of the new rifled naval cannon, steam propulsion, and armor plating. This was one area in which the Confederacy could compete on equal terms. During the course of the war the Confederate navy began construction of nearly 50 ironclads, of which 22 were put into commission.

The CSS *Virginia*

By far the most famous ironclad was the CSS *Virginia*. This ship was adapted from the hulk of the frigate USS *Merrimack*, which had been only partly destroyed

Commerce raiding

The capture of Union merchant vessels at sea to disrupt the North's ability to trade.

Curriculum Context

Students might be asked to discuss the effect of technological innovation on the course of the war.

when the Norfolk naval yard was abandoned by Union forces. It mounted ten 11-inch (25-cm) cannons and an iron ram on the bow below the waterline.

The *Virginia* briefly struck terror in Union hearts. During its maiden voyage on March 8, 1862, it steamed from Norfolk into Hampton Roads, Virginia, destroying two Union warships and disabling a third. The next day it steamed forth only to be met by an oddly shaped vessel. This was the USS *Monitor*, the Union's own ironclad. The *Monitor* successfully neutralized the *Virginia*; but even if it had failed to do so, it is difficult to see how much more damage the Confederate ironclad could inflict. The *Virginia* was too unseaworthy to sail beyond the protected waters of Hampton Roads and drew too much water to steam up to the Potomac River and Washington, D.C. Just two months after its duel with the *Monitor* the *Virginia* had to be scuttled to prevent its capture. The *Virginia* epitomized the problems of Confederate ironclads. They were slow, unwieldy, and suffered from many mechanical defects.

Coastal defenses

To defend their ports, the Confederates used sea mines (then called torpedoes). These explosive charges could damage or sink any ship they came into contact with. Union Admiral David G. Farragut's famous cry "Damn the torpedoes! Go ahead!" at the Battle of Mobile Bay in August 1864 was made just after he saw one of his ships sunk by a torpedo. A torpedo could also be attached to a long spar mounted on a small, fast, unarmored vessel. The spar would hit an enemy vessel, and the torpedo would explode, but the torpedo boat itself usually survived with little or no damage.

Blockade-runners and commerce raiders

To evade the Union naval blockade of Southern ports, the Confederacy took advantage of blockade-runners—fast, steam-driven vessels often specifically

---

Drew

Sank too deeply in the water to pass over the riverbed.

Spar

A long, rounded spear projecting from something.

Blockade

A barrier of warships and defenses intended to prevent trade.

designed to outrun patrol ships. Many were privately owned and their captains preferred to carry cargos of luxury goods, so the Confederate navy commissioned 43 of its own blockade-runners to ensure military essentials got through to sustain the war effort.

The Confederacy briefly tried using privateers, a kind of legalized piracy in which a government gave private vessels permission to capture enemy shipping. As the Union blockade became more effective, captains found it too difficult to bring captured prizes into Southern ports, which was the only way to make privateering pay. As a result, the Confederacy turned to commerce raiders with regular naval crews that were designed to destroy, not capture, enemy merchantmen.

The Confederate commerce raiders achieved great notoriety and in some cases great effectiveness. Many commerce raiders were built in England, secretly commissioned by a Confederate agent in London, James Bulloch. (He also tried to get ironclads built in Britain but was blocked by the British government.) Commerce raiders sank a large number of Union merchantmen, forced hundreds more to seek refuge by reregistering under neutral flags, and sent insurance

The Confederate ironclad CSS *Virginia* rammed and sank the wooden frigate USS *Cumberland* in the Battle of Hampton Roads, Virginia, on March 8, 1862. The engagement showed that wooden ships were no match for the new ironclads.

Curriculum Context

Do you think that the tactic of commerce raiding deserved to earn notoriety? Was it a legitimate tactic of warfare?

premiums soaring. The commerce raider CSS *Shenandoah*, for example, managed to cripple the New England whaling fleet in the Bering Sea: although it did not achieve this until June 1865, unaware that the war was over.

Effectiveness of the navy

Although Mallory did a superb job of creating a navy—he even set up a naval academy to train new officers—it must be questioned whether that navy achieved results worth even the relatively slender resources spent on it. The ironclad program produced several formidable vessels, but they usually failed to prevent Union warships from capturing a Southern port when they mounted a major effort to do so. Land fortifications, not armored vessels, seemed the most effective way to defend Southern harbors. The commerce raiders, for their part, did considerable damage, but never enough to deflate the North's will to continue the war. Considering the vast amount of commerce carried by Northern ships, the raiders were really little more than a nuisance.

Curriculum Context

You might be asked to assess the effectiveness of Southern tactics; the progress of the naval war might be a useful point to discuss.

Adventures of the *Alabama*

The greatest Southern commerce raider was the CSS *Alabama*, commanded by Captain Raphael Semmes. Built in England, the *Alabama* mounted eight guns and could reach a speed of more than 13 knots under steam. Starting in August 1862, it destroyed 68 Union vessels in 22 months—without injuring the crews. The sailors boarded the enemy merchantmen and took their seamen prisoner before destroying the vessels. When the *Alabama* grew too crowded, Semmes would designate the next captured merchantman a "cartel ship," place the prisoners on board, and let

them sail to the nearest port. In that way he accomplished his mission without bloodshed.

The *Alabama*'s colorful career lasted until June 1864, when the Union frigate USS *Kearsarge* cornered the raider in the port of Cherbourg, France. The *Kearsarge* waited outside the port, barring escape. The *Alabama* came forth to fight but was sunk in a spirited one-hour engagement. Semmes himself went over the side. He was picked up by the *Deerhound*, a yacht filled with admiring sightseers, who helped him escape capture by taking him to England.

Desertion

Desertion was a major problem for both sides. An estimated one in every seven Union soldiers and one in every nine Confederate soldiers left their posts without permission for one reason or another, and did not return to service.

Many of the reasons for desertion were common to both armies. The most obvious reason—cowardice—was by no means the main one. More influential was the lack of such necessities as food, clothing, and equipment. Other important factors included battle fatigue andzeral despondency at the course and duration of the war. A significant number of soldiers deserted because they did not believe in the cause. Numerous others resented the coercion, both of themselves and others. Yet more soldiers were worried about their loved ones back home.

Curriculum Context

If you are asked to consider the motives for desertion, it is important to remember that cowardice was far from the only one.

Union deserters

Conditions in the Union army were bad. Some of the adversities—the fear of dying, the low morale after a defeat, the boredom caused by military routine—were foreseeable consequences of war, but others were particular to the Civil War. One was the shortage of arms, which undermined their morale. Thirst,

Union General Marsena R. Patrick, provost marshal of the Army of the Potomac, and his staff in Culpeper, Virginia, 1863. The army provost marshal was in charge of discovering and punishing deserters.

starvation, extreme heat, and disease were rife. The men were often further demoralized by lack of confidence in their commanders and by the habitual delays in payment.

Curriculum Context

Would soldiers in the mid-19th century be any more likely to lack self-discipline than people today?

Many soldiers made active decisions to desert. Others simply got lost as an army moved across country, and they were neither well trained nor motivated enough to find their way back. A small but significant minority simply lacked the self-discipline needed for life in the armed forces.

In December 1862 it was estimated that a total of 180,000 Union soldiers were absent, either with or without leave. Although there are no authoritative figures for the number of Union deserters, the consensus among modern historians is that there were more than 200,000 deserters from the Union army, including nearly 45,000 from New York, more than 24,000 from Pennsylvania, and 18,000 from Ohio.

Ways of deserting

The chief method of desertion was to take sick leave or a furlough (leave of absence) to go away and never return. Others deserted by straggling (slipping to the rear during a march or in battle) or by offering themselves for capture to the enemy, who treated them honorably. A large number of deserters actually changed sides. Union deserters resurfaced in a variety of locations. Absenteeism from the ranks cost the North victories and undoubtedly prolonged the war.

Absenteeism

Being absent from duty without permission.

Confederate deserters

Many of the privations of Union armies were the same in the Confederate armies. In addition, the Confederate army had many conscripts—among them Northerners and Mexicans—who had no interest in the Southern cause and no sympathy for slavery. When conditions became intolerable, they were the first to desert.

Conscripts

People who are forced to join an army without any individual choice.

Punishing Deserters

The maximum penalty for desertion was capital punishment. Although the death sentence was sometimes carried out, many generals were soon forced to start treating desertion more as a breach of contract than as a grave crime. They made public appeals to deserters, offering pardons to those who returned voluntarily and warning of dire consequences for those who did not. This was a practical policy rather than an expression of principle—there were simply too many deserters to execute them all. Although the number of executions increased after 1863, they were no more than token gestures to encourage the fainthearted. A few men were used as examples, while thousands of others who were equally guilty went unpunished.

After the war ended, despite a law stating clearly that only soldiers who had been honorably discharged were eligible for pensions, Congress passed many private and special acts that "corrected" the military record. The heroism of many soldiers was fabricated retrospectively.

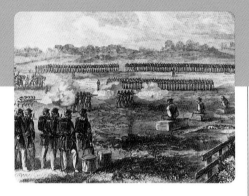

Confederate wages were sometimes as many as 14 months late, and army camps were notorious for their lack of sanitation. In some parts of the South the fear of Native Americans on scalping tours was greater than that of Union soldiers. A mere rumor that Indians were in the area was enough to provoke large-scale desertions. Many of the camp followers who tagged along behind the armies were profiteering at the soldiers' expense, and this lowered morale.

Desertion was widespread. There is some anecdotal evidence that whole companies decamped at the same time. The Confederate army punished deserters, but the decision of the high command to send soldiers in pursuit of deserters reduced the numbers available to fight in battles and contributed greatly to the final defeat of the Confederacy. Of the deserters who were captured, few were executed because the army needed every man it could get.

An illustration from *Harper's Weekly*, August 1863, showing the execution of deserters from the Union Army of the Potomac. Although desertion was widespread, few deserters were executed.

Discipline, Military

Maintaining military discipline was a problem for both sides throughout the Civil War. This was not because volunteer soldiers were deliberately disobedient, but more that military order and discipline did not come naturally to them.

Curriculum Context

Army commanders had discovered through history that it was easier to get men to fight through loyalty to their regiment or companions than through loyalty to an abstract cause, such as patriotism.

Subordination

The state of being junior to someone else.

The disciplinary problem had its roots in the way the armies were raised in 1861. Regiments were mustered in local neighborhoods from volunteers. True to their democratic heritage, these men had chosen their own officers by a vote among themselves and expected to be led in a way that everyone agreed with.

Instilling discipline

To the officers who had served in the old regular army this was a recipe for chaos. Union officer Ulysses S. Grant found his regiment in just such a state on taking up his first command as the new colonel of the 21st Illinois in 1861 but set about instilling discipline in his men by making them work very hard. As Grant recognized, it was the soldier's subordination to his officer and the ability to follow orders that were key to unit discipline. Too many of the officers in the new volunteer armies tried to control their men by making friends with them. This was disastrous, as the rout of the Union army at the first battle of the war on July 21, 1861, at Bull Run (Manassas) was to prove.

Discipline started to sharpen up after that defeat as poor-quality volunteer officers were transferred or removed, and men of Grant's experience and caliber began to rise to more senior levels of command.

It was not just an unwillingness to obey orders that caused bad discipline in the ranks. As one Iowa private wrote, "There is no mistake, but the majority of soldiers are a hard set." Such men inevitably got into trouble.

Common breaches of army regulations included drunkenness, sleeping while on duty, fighting, and theft from other soldiers. The result of such behavior would be a company punishment decided on by the officer in charge. The type of punishment varied widely from unit to unit and depended on the officer and the company's state of discipline.

Serious offenses

Offenses such as cowardice or desertion were too serious to be dealt with at company level. They came under the jurisdiction of the provost marshal, the army's police service. The provost guards patrolled behind the battle lines. Soldiers caught leaving the field could be sent for court-martial, a formal hearing chaired by at least three officers. It was here that the severest penalties were given out. Punishments included branding by hot iron on the hand, cheek, or thigh and flogging. Although flogging had been officially abolished in the U.S. Army before the war, it was used in the Confederate army until 1863.

Court martial
A military court.

Flogging
To beat on the back with a whip or a thin wooden rod.

Camp Punishments

Minor breaches of discipline such as fighting or drunkenness could be met by confinement to the guardhouse and rations of bread and water for several days. Harsher penalties of the types Grant described as "a little regular army punishment" were designed to shame, humiliate, and at their most extreme inflict pain on the wrongdoer.

A drunk could be given hard labor and forced to stand on a barrel with a bottle of whiskey around his neck. Thieves were made to march around camp or stand on a wooden barrel wearing a sign saying "Thief."

Making soldiers carry heavy weights such as logs or iron rails around camp for hours was also common. Another punishment was making a soldier wear a ball and chain clamped to his leg. The iron ball could weigh 12 pounds (5.4 kg) or even 32 pounds (14.5 kg).

A soldier might be "bucked and gagged" for more serious breaches of discipline. This involved the soldier sitting on the ground for hours with his hands tied around his bended knees with a gag placed in his mouth. There were also incidences of men being tied up by their thumbs.

A sketch by Alfred Waud showing the punishment for gamblers in the Army of the Potomac. Many camp punishments involved humiliating the offender by making them wear signs, such as "gambler," "drunk," or "coward."

Mutiny

An organized or large-scale revolt against military orders.

The severest punishment of all was the death penalty. It was the sentence for cases of murder, rape, and mutiny. Desertion could also result in the death penalty, especially when it threatened to become widespread in an army and a serious threat to discipline and morale. The Army of Northern Virginia, for example, executed 31 men for desertion in the last six months of the war.

Witnessing executions

Execution was usually by firing squad, although some people were hanged. The sentence was carried out in public in front of the condemned soldier's unit. His regiment, or even the entire brigade, was paraded to witness the execution, not only as a final humiliation of the condemned man but also a blunt warning from the military authorities to the rest of the soldiery.

Curriculum Context

Army commanders wanted to ensure that soldiers who fled from possible death knew that they faced a worse fate: certain death.

Soldiers ordered to witness an execution often found it the most distressing experience of their war service. An eyewitness recalled the reaction in one such unit: "It was hard to bear. Faces paled and hands shook which were not accustomed to show fear: and officers and men alike would have welcomed a call to battle in exchange for that terrible inaction in the sight of coming death."

Engineering, Military

The Corps of Engineers was one of the most important branches of service in the armies of both sides. Engineers were responsible for building fortifications and trench systems and for constructing and repairing roads and bridges.

Engineers were responsible for surveying terrain to find possible routes of march and for preparing accurate maps for commanding generals. Both of these tasks were vital because the United States at the time of the Civil War was largely unmapped. The armies had to maneuver and fight over large areas of country with few roads, while bridges, if they existed at all, were frequently destroyed by enemy action. The military engineer's role was so important that in the years before the Civil War the top graduates of the U.S. Military Academy at West Point were usually posted to the Corps of Engineers. Several of the war's leading generals from both sides began their military careers in this way, including Confederate Generals Robert E. Lee and Pierre G. T. Beauregard, and the Union commander at Gettysburg, George G. Meade.

Union engineers

At the beginning of the war Union engineers were organized into two separate departments, the Corps of Engineers, who were the builders and diggers, and the Corps of Topographical Engineers, who were the surveyors and mappers. Once the Union army gained experience of campaigning, it found the two engineer departments worked so closely together it made sense to combine them.

Members of the corps

The men who served in the corps were a mixture of regular army officers, officers and men who had signed up as volunteers, and civilian contractors.

Curriculum Context

Some curricula ask students to discuss the role of geography on the development of the United States, including on the causes and outcome of the Civil War.

Topographical

Concerned with representing places on maps or in charts.

Curriculum Context

Siege warfare required the besieging force to dig rings of fortifications from which to fire artillery shells into the besieged town.

There had been a construction boom in the 1840s and 1850s that had created a sizable pool of experienced surveyors and engineers, but such men were always in short supply in the Union army during the war. During the Siege of Vicksburg, Mississippi, in 1863, Union General Ulysses S. Grant commanded an army of 70,000 men but was able to call on the services of only three engineer officers to oversee the construction of his trenches. The only way to solve the shortage was for the men of the line regiments to become involved—a task they proved willing to take on.

Large-scale projects

Military engineering projects were often on a huge scale. One of the first and biggest was the defense system built around Washington, D.C., to ward off any possible Confederate attack from Virginia. By the end of the war 20 miles (32 km) of trenches and 68 forts and artillery emplacements ringed the capital. One of Grant's early attempts to take Vicksburg involved 4,000 men digging a mile-long canal through a bend of the Mississippi River. The project took nine months to complete between June 1862 and March 1863.

Sieges of other Confederate cities were just as hard and long drawn out. Union forces battered away at the defenses around Charleston, South Carolina, for two

This bridge on the Orange and Alexandria Railroad in Virginia was repaired by troops under Colonel Herman Haupt, the engineer in charge of all Union military railroads.

The Mine at Petersburg

During the Siege of Petersburg, Virginia, in June 1864 the Union troops of the 48th Pennsylvania Infantry were stuck in trenches and frustrated at being unable to get at the enemy. The regiment was made up of former coal miners, and the soldiers came up with the idea of digging a tunnel under the enemy lines, planting gunpowder at the end of it, and blowing up one of the Confederate forts.

The army engineers initially declared their plan impossible since they would have to dig a tunnel more than 500 feet (150 m), and no mine had ever been dug so far. However, the commanding officer, Colonel Henry Pleasants, who had himself been a mining engineer before the war, believed in the idea. He managed to persuade his corps commander, Ambrose E. Burnside, of its worth and soon had the entire regiment at work on the project.

Using improvised tools, the 48th Pennsylvania dug a tunnel 511 feet (156 m) long into which was packed 4 tons (3.6 tonnes) of gunpowder. When it was detonated on July 30, the explosion blasted a crater in the Confederate lines nearly 200 feet (61 m) long, 30 feet (9.1 m) deep, and 60 feet (18.2 m) wide, which is visible to this day.

and a half years before its surrender in February 1865. During the nine-month Siege of Petersburg the Confederate Army of Northern Virginia held a trench line over 12 miles (19 km) long until they were finally forced out in April 1865.

Confederate Engineer Corps

The Confederate Corps of Engineers was always at a disadvantage because of the smaller number of men and amount of resources it could employ, which makes its achievements even more remarkable. In 1861 the Confederate army had only a small number of professional military engineers, officers who had formerly served with the U.S. Army. They were joined by trained volunteers and by civilian contractors paid by the government. The number of professional engineers in the Confederate army was so low that only one or two could be posted to each corps. Extra manpower had to come from the line regiments, with men being temporarily drafted from the ranks to do the work of pioneers, the laborers of the army.

Contractors

Employers, such as construction workers, who accept a contract to provide a particular service.

Union engineers building a corduroy road near Richmond, Virginia, during the Peninsular Campaign, June 1862.

Unlike the Union engineers, the Confederate Engineer Corps combined the roles of construction, surveying, and mapmaking into one organization from the beginning. It was also an officer-only corps until 1863, when conscription brought more qualified and experienced men into the service. That allowed for the establishment of two engineer regiments of 1,000 officers and men, each 10 companies strong. Like their Union counterparts, these new engineer companies were attached to an army headquarters and led by a brigadier general.

Keeping the army moving

Military engineers were credited with being able to overcome any obstacle if they were so ordered—even keeping an army advancing when it faced a trackless wilderness and broad rivers. Engineers surveyed routes through unmapped country and built roads to carry the armies through. These roads were temporary constructions called corduroy roads made from logs that were laid down in two layers and covered in packed earth.

Corduroy roads

Log roads, named for their resemblance to the ridges on corduroy fabric.

Pontoon bridge

A temporary bridge that often floats on a shallow boat named a pontoon.

Crossing a river without any existing bridge or fording place was a complex operation. Portable pontoon bridges were transported with the army in a train of up to 35 horse-drawn wagons. The wagons carried the pontoons—wooden flat-bottomed boats up to 30 feet (9 m) long—and wooden balks, which were long timbers tied end to end from pontoon to pontoon to provide a stable foundation for the bridge's surface. The surface was made by laying large planks called chesses side by side across the balks.

Bridging operations

The Union Army of the Potomac became expert at laying and taking up pontoon bridges. All of its operations in northern Virginia were dominated by the need to get men and supplies over the many rivers and creeks that separated the Maryland border on the Potomac River from the Confederate capital, Richmond, Virginia, on the James River. Some of these bridging operations were huge. On December 11, 1862, Union army engineers began work on six pontoon bridges across the Rappahannock River at Fredericksburg. Despite a delay in the arrival of the pontoons and heavy Confederate fire, the task was completed in one day, allowing the Army of the Potomac's Grand Divisions to cross in force and fight the Battle of Fredericksburg two days later on December 13, 1862.

The Swamp Angel

One of the greatest feats of engineering during the war was the construction of a battery specially built to shell Charleston, South Carolina, during the Union siege of the Confederate-held city.

Union commander Quincy A. Gillmore surveyed the marshes around Morris Island in Charleston Harbor. He then ordered a battery to be built on the marsh that could support the combined weight of a gun and carriage of 24,000 pounds (10,890 kg).

Working at night to avoid Confederate fire, the Union troops built a platform by driving pilings through 18 feet (5.5 m) of mud. On top of the platform they built a parapet made from 13,000 sandbags. Finally in position on August 17, the 200-pounder (90-kg) Parrott gun was sighted on the steeple of St Michael's Church in Charleston. It then shelled the city from nearly 8,000 yards (7.3 km) away. The Swamp Angel, as the gun was dubbed, fired 36 shells before it exploded on August 23. It had fired shells farther than any previous piece of artillery.

The Union shelling of Charleston was one of the first examples of a civilian target being picked to achieve a military aim. The Confederate authorities protested against the Union action.

Fortifications

The Civil War was marked by a large number of battles and sieges fought in and around fortifications. Towns and cities were ringed with trenches and forts, and sometimes whole armies were besieged behind lines of entrenchments.

The conflict began in 1861 over a fort—Fort Sumter in Charleston Harbor—and as the war went on, both sides made greater and greater use of fortified positions against the enemy. Cities and towns were ringed with trenches and forts, and on occasions whole armies were besieged behind lines of entrenchments. At the outbreak of the war it was not the threat from opposing armies that created the need for fortifications but the danger posed by enemy navies. In 1861 the newest and strongest forts in the United States were designed to defend the Atlantic seaports from possible attack by foreign warships.

Fort Sumter in Charleston Harbor, South Carolina, and Fort Pulaski off Savannah, Georgia, were two such forts. They were constructed of masonry and brick with walls 5 feet (1.5 m) thick, strong enough to withstand a pounding by the large-caliber smoothbore cannon carried on board battleships. The forts held permanent garrisons of men in specially built barracks who served the fort's own defensive armament: the big seacoast guns, the smallest of which could fire a 32-pound (14.5-kg) iron cannonball over a mile (1.6 km).

The Confederacy's first concern was the naval threat along its vast network of navigable rivers, which provided vital routes for commerce and trade. To defend the rivers, the Confederates built forts at key points. They were semipermanent structures with earth banks up to 20 feet (8 m) high reinforced with tree trunks, sandbags, or even layers of railroad iron.

Entrenchments

Defensive trenches dug into the ground, often protected by earthworks.

Curriculum Context

The course of the war was to a large extent dictated by the need to control the rivers.

Increased fortifications

The sheer size of the country over which the armies fought made it impossible for either side to have soldiers everywhere. The Confederacy was fighting a defensive war to protect new borders that stretched over thousands of miles and had to rely on garrisons in lightly manned forts to protect large areas.

Garrison

A unit of soldiers based in a stronghold in order to defend a particular town or area.

Fortified cities

Cities became strategic targets for attack, so fortifications were constructed to defend them. One of the first actions of the Union War Department was to defend Washington, D.C., with a massive system of trenches over 20 miles (32 km) long supported by 68 artillery forts to deter a Confederate attack. The Union army meanwhile besieged many cities in the South. New Orleans, Atlanta, Charleston, and the capital, Richmond, were attacked and eventually captured.

The most famous Union siege was at Vicksburg, Mississippi. Between May and July 1863 Vicksburg endured continual assaults from Grant's Union force of more than 70,000 men and 200 guns. Under a constant bombardment that destroyed buildings and killed people indiscriminately, the city's population was forced underground to live in caves dug out of the hillside, turning the city into a warren that the Union soldiers referred to as "the prairie dogs' village."

An elaborate system of trenches in the Union lines during the Siege of Petersburg, Virginia (June 1864–April 1865). The trenches became more complex and better protected as the siege went on.

River Forts

The Confederacy's first concern after the outbreak of war was also to defend itself from the naval threat. The threat came not so much to its coastline—Confederate forces had captured many of the Atlantic seacoast forts, such as Fort Sumter, to defend against that—but to its vast network of navigable rivers, particularly in the West. In 1861 these rivers included the Mississippi River from south of Illinois to the delta, together with tributaries such as the Cumberland and the Tennessee rivers.

The rivers provided vital routes for commerce and trade between the Confederate states, but also created a direct route into the heartland of the South for Union gunboats and transport vessels full of Federal troops, if they could fight their way through.

Forts were built overlooking the rivers at strategic points. These new forts were large, semipermanent structures with earth banks up to 20 feet (6 m) high reinforced with tree trunks, sandbags, or even layers of railroad iron, behind which were big artillery guns and large garrisons of infantry posted in rifle pits. In Tennessee, for example, Fort Donelson on the Cumberland River covered an area of 100 acres (40 ha), but was considered small by attacking Union troops. The fort was situated on a bend in the river that it could sweep with nine batteries of guns, including one massive 128-pounder (58 kg) cannon.

New weapons

The range and killing power of the latest infantry weapons made it obvious that the safest place on a battlefield was behind cover. Once protected from fire, defenders could then use these same weapons to attack. Some of the war's costliest assaults took place in front of hastily improvised positions. A sunken road and wooden fence near Sharpsburg, Maryland, became known as Bloody Lane after an afternoon of slaughter at Antietam in September 1862, while a stone wall along Marye's Heights provided enough protection for 6,000 Confederates to fight off assaults by 40,000 Union troops in the Battle of Fredericksburg in Virginia the following December.

Battlefield positions

Having experienced terrible examples of what the latest weaponry could do, by 1864 soldiers would protect themselves. If a short halt in the march was

Curriculum Context

In some Civil War battles it is possible to pinpoint a precise point, like Bloody Lane at Antietam or the Hornets' Nest at Shiloh, where the course of the whole battle was decided.

called, soldiers dug rifle pits (now known as foxholes); if an army halted for more than a day, troops built lines of entrenchments to protect themselves.

The Siege of Petersburg, Virginia of June 1864 began with the armies of Confederate General Robert E. Lee and Union General Ulysses S. Grant digging trenches that eventually surrounded both Lee's army and the city. Such systems began as simple battlefield defenses; but as the months went by, they grew, becoming semipermanent networks of trenches and larger structures called fieldworks. They had bombproofs, which were reinforced dugouts designed to shelter men against shell and mortar fire, as well as gun emplacements for artillery and redoubts (small forts) to defend against attack. The strength of the Confederate defenses at Petersburg defeated Grant's attempts to break Lee's hold on the city for 10 months. Grant then launched massive assaults that shattered the Confederate lines. As shortages of men and supplies took their toll, Lee was forced to retreat in April 1865.

Curriculum Context

Curricula might ask you to describe key battles of the war: Grant's victory at Petersburg meant that it was now impossible for Lee to continue to defend the Confederate capital, Richmond, Virginia.

Defensive obstacles

Civil War troops protected fieldwork positions by placing obstacles in front of them. They included chevaux-de-frise (logs fitted with pointed stakes) and gabions (wicker baskets packed with earth). Union General Ambrose E. Burnside is said to have introduced wire entanglements strung along the ground to trip up attackers—a forerunner to the later developments of barbed wire and razor wire.

Trench warfare

Fighting in trenches introduced a new type of warfare. Gone were the days of marching behind regimental colors and volley fire by rank. Now there was the endless building and mending of trenches and the nerve-racking business of dodging the sharpshooter's bullet and the random flight of a mortar shell.

Sharpshooter

A marksman whose task was to pick off individual enemy soldiers, often at distance, using highly accurate rifle fire.

Guerrilla Warfare

While armies clashed on the battlefield, a different kind of war raged throughout the Confederacy, the Union border states, and Indian Territory. Guerrilla tactics were used by cavalry raiders, partisans, and independent lawless bands.

Curriculum Context

Some curricula might expect students to understand reasons for the Union attitude toward civilians in the Southern territory it captured.

Union forces everywhere had to contend with secessionist guerrillas, whose activities took the form of ambushes, raids, and outright murder. Frustration with the guerrillas helped harden the Union government's attitude toward Southern civilians. The Confederate government had its share of pro-Union guerrillas to contend with and adopted a similarly harsh policy toward many Southern Unionists.

The term "guerrilla" derives from the Spanish word for "little war." The guerrilla style of fighting was well known, especially from the American Revolution, when famous partisans such as Francis Marion had attacked British supply trains and outposts. Many Americans associated guerrilla warfare with adventure, romance, and bold deeds. The reality proved to be very different.

Partisans

Guerrilla fighters operating behind enemy lines.

Guerrilla tactics

There were three distinct groups who used guerrilla tactics. The first group were regular cavalrymen. Two famous examples were the Confederate generals John H. Morgan and Nathan B. Forrest. Although they often moved and fought in an elusive, hit-and-run manner like guerrillas, both they and their troops wore uniforms, carried their weapons openly, and were part of large, regularly organized military units.

Curriculum Context

Forrest's exploits made him a great hero of the Confederacy; he was one of the South's leading military commanders.

The second group were partisan rangers. Although independent, these units operated with the formal sanction of the Confederate government. The most famous of these units was John S. Mosby's 43rd

Partisan Battalion, which carried out raids in northern Virginia. They wore uniforms and carried weapons openly but seldom engaged in stand-up battles. When they were not actively engaged, most of them hid their uniforms and weapons.

The third, much larger category, was self-constituted bands of guerrillas that operated without government authorization. They usually wore civilian attire and hid their weapons. They sabotaged trains and ambushed isolated parties of enemy troops. They also intimidated, assaulted, or even killed civilians who held political views different from their own. In parts of Tennessee prosecessionist guerrillas prevented an election called by the Union military governor, while in Missouri pro-Union guerrillas terrorized Confederate sympathizers.

Government attitudes

Both governments recognized the legitimacy of guerrilla tactics when used by uniformed combatants who carried their weapons openly. Both sides thought those who did not were bandits, who were subject to military trial and execution if they were caught. In practice they were sometimes executed on the spot.

Sabotage

To destroy key property or otherwise interfere with an enemy's ability to operate.

Curriculum Context

Do you think that those who do not play by the "rules" of war should expect to be subject to such punishments?

Guerrilla Atrocities

Part of the testimony of Miss Lavinia Piles at the trial of the Tennessee guerrilla Champ Furguson:

"I was at my fathers house in October, 1862, when Furguson and his gang came there. It was just after daybreak. . . . They brought John Williams, John Crabtree, and David Delk with them. They were all tied together by their arms.

"They entered the gate, and came into the yard near the stables, taking the prisoners with them. One of them came back and told us to go in the house. We did so, and heard three guns fired near the stable. One of them came back and told us they had killed the prisoners. We then went out, and they passed on out the gate.

"We found the dead bodies of the boys lying near the stable. Mr. Williams was shot three times under his right ear, in his right arm, and in the breast. Delk was stabbed under the right arm. Crabtree was cut to pieces. . . . in Delk's shoulder, a corn stalk was stuck in the wound."

It was very common for Union and Confederate troops to seize hostages, burn houses, or seize goods belonging to civilians in a bid to stamp out guerrilla activity.

Famous guerrillas

Morgan and Mosby spawned a romantic legend of guerrillas as "gray ghosts and rebel raiders," but the true nature of guerrilla war found its expression in the exploits of vicious men such as Charles R. Jennison, William C. Quantrill, and Champ Furguson. They fought largely in Missouri, the state that probably saw the most widespread and intensive guerrilla struggle. A product of the prewar "Bleeding Kansas" violence of the 1850s, Jennison and his Jayhawkers used the Civil War as an opportunity to retaliate against the "border ruffians" who had narrowly failed to make Kansas a slave state. They plundered homes, stole livestock, and looted several towns.

Bands of secessionists formed to deal with the Union Jayhawkers and their sympathizers. William C. Quantrill became the foremost leader of these secessionist guerrillas. A controversial figure, he was declared an outlaw by the Union but received a captaincy in the Confederate army. Among those who fought in his band were Frank and Jesse James and "Bloody Bill" Anderson. Quantrill and his men adopted a policy of "no quarter" with regard to both Jayhawkers and Union soldiers, which meant that they killed any who were unlucky enough to fall into their hands. After a year of raids in Missouri, on August 21, 1863, Quantrill's men attacked Lawrence, Kansas, well known as a hotbed of antislavery sentiment. On Quantrill's orders they burned the town and murdered every adult male they

An illustration in *Harpers' Weekly* of Confederate partisan raider John S. Mosby and his band attacking a sutlers' wagon train in September 1863.

Frank and Jesse James

The James brothers led a notorious criminal gang in the Wild West after the Civil War.

encountered, as well as a small garrison of Union soldiers. In all, more than 150 people were killed and 200 dwellings destroyed.

Jennison and Quantrill were unusual in that they each commanded a large body of followers. Champ Furguson was more typical. A Tennessee man, he led small groups of bushwhackers in the Cumberland highlands, sometimes fighting alone. He is believed to have killed more than a hundred men during the war, often with great cruelty. The postwar U.S. government refused to grant him amnesty. Instead, he was tried and executed as an outlaw.

The "guerrilla option"

In early 1865, as it became clear the Confederate armies would soon lose, a few Southerners began to call for a resort to guerrilla warfare. Union commanders such as Ulysses S. Grant and William T. Sherman feared the Confederates might embrace this "guerrilla option." Confederate General Robert E. Lee, who was very skeptical of the value of guerrilla warfare, specifically warned President Davis against it in his final dispatch after his surrender at Appomattox, Virginia, in April 1865: "A partisan war may be continued, and hostilities protracted, causing individual suffering and the devastation of the country, but I see no prospect by that means of achieving a separate independence."

Although the Confederacy rejected the guerrilla option, in the postwar period white Southerners employed something very like it. Their goal was to reassert control over Southern state governments. Paramilitary organizations, such as the Ku Klux Klan and the Knights of the White Camelia, conducted campaigns of intimidation, riot, and murder in a bid to eliminate the Republican Party as a significant force in the South and to force African Americans to accept political, social, and economic domination by whites.

Curriculum Context

When considering significant moments of the war, it might be useful to consider an atrocity such as Quantrill's Raid.

Amnesty

A pardon granted by a government.

Curriculum Context

The use of guerrilla movements in the South should be considered by anyone studying the South during Reconstruction.

Horses

Civil War armies used horses in their hundreds of thousands. Before the introduction of motorized transportation in the 20th century armies depended on horses for supplies, swift movement in battle, and to maneuver artillery.

Horses had many roles during the war. Cavalrymen charged and fought on horseback, scouts rode ahead of their units, and officers were mounted as a symbol of their rank. Artillery batteries used teams of horses to pull guns and carry ammunition, and the armies relied on horses to help transport supplies.

Transporting supplies

The bulk of army supplies were hauled by railroad and riverboat to collection depots. From there the supplies were transported in wagons pulled by horses or mules to the battle fronts. On campaign the wagon train followed behind the troops. During General Ulysses S. Grant's invasion of Virginia in 1864 the Army of the Potomac had a wagon train over 5 miles (8 km) long, drawn by 500 horses. The task of maintaining an army relied on the regular supply of horses.

Confederate horses

Throughout the war the Confederate army relied on its soldiers, especially its cavalrymen, to provide their own mounts. There was no official organization to keep its army supplied with mounts. As the fighting dragged on, horses in the South were in short supply. By July 1864 General Robert E. Lee was so worried about the lack of cavalry horses that he wrote to President Jefferson Davis suggesting horses could be purchased in Texas. They would then swim across the Mississippi River before being driven the 1,200 miles (1,920 km) to Virginia. Lee realized that the journey would be arduous, but urged Davis to consider the plan.

Curriculum Context

The need for so many horses for the war effort meant that there was a shortage of horses left for farm work at home.

Union horses

During the early years of war the Union government did not think about the future supply of horses. It was not until July 1863 that it set up the Cavalry Bureau to buy and distribute horses. The biggest Union horse depot, at Giesboro near Washington, D.C., covered 600 acres and had stockyards, stables, and forage warehouses to keep 30,000 animals. By 1865 the Union government had spent $124 million supplying its army with mounts. On campaign even this well-organized system occasionally failed. As Union armies invaded the Southern states, they were tempted simply to take the horses they needed. Robert E. Lee's sorrel mare, Lucy Long, was stolen near the end of the war. She was found after the surrender and returned to Lee.

Medical care

The average life expectancy of horses in Civil War service was six months. Cavalry mounts were killed or wounded by enemy fire, transport animals died from overwork, and many horses died from disease, exposure and poor forage in the winter. By July 1863 Lee's army included more than 6,000 recuperating horses. In the following month the Union army began appointing a veterinary surgeon for every cavalry regiment. Such efforts did not prevent the total deaths of horses and mules in the two armies climbing to an estimated 1.5 million by the end of the war.

Forage
Food for animals.

Sorrel
A reddish–chestnut, which is a common color in horses.

A blacksmith's forge used by the Union Army of the Potomac during the Siege of Petersburg in Virginia (June 1864–April 1865).

Infantry Tactics

Infantry tactics changed considerably during the course of the Civil War. Changes were brought about by the introduction of new weapons, especially the rifled musket, which had a greater range and accuracy than previous weapons.

Both sides used similar battle tactics during the Civil War since many generals had been taught at the same military schools and had served together in the U.S. Army before the war. Their field officers, who led the men into combat, were mostly volunteers. They had to learn battle maneuvers from books, such as *Hardee's Tactics*, a manual widely read by officers on both sides.

The objective of infantry tactics was to maneuver units of troops into a position as quickly and efficiently as possible, so as to bring the maximum amount of musket fire to bear onto the enemy and then to charge with bayonets and drive the enemy from the field. In July 1861, Confederate commander Thomas "Stonewall" Jackson's brigade broke the Union attack on Henry Hill using exactly these tactics in the First Battle of Bull Run (Manassas).

Training and drill

Infantry companies were trained to march in column, usually four men across. On an order they could change formation and direction and, without altering pace, deploy into a battle line two ranks deep 16 inches (40 cm) apart, facing the enemy. They were then ordered to load and fire their muskets. A regiment had to retain its coordination in battle to be effective. Constant training and drill were needed to accomplish this, in addition to strictly following the orders shouted by officers or signaled by bugle calls or drums. This method of getting large numbers of men into combat was adaptable enough to allow infantry units of any

Curriculum Context

Students asked to describe key interventions by individuals might include Jackson's famous stand on Henry Hill, when the discipline of his infantry in the face of a Union onslaught earned him his nickname; a fellow officer encouraged his own men, saying, "There is Jackson standing like a stone wall."

size to deploy for action using the same maneuvers. A regiment could form a line by deploying its companies and a brigade by deploying its regiments.

The battle line did not form a solid wall of soldiers. To allow room for maneuver, the manuals recommended a 20-yard (18.5-m) gap between regiments and a 25-yard (23-m) gap between brigades. Regiments could also hold companies behind the line in reserve or advance companies forward in a skirmish line up to 500 yards (450 m) ahead of the main formation. Skirmishers operated in "open order," each man spaced a few yards from the next, taking advantage of any cover to keep the enemy line under fire. Skirmishers also maintained contact with the enemy and gave warning if they began to move forward for an attack.

Method of attack

The most common method of attack was to advance lines of regiments or brigades one after the other in waves about 25 yards (23 m) apart. Often the first wave was used as cover for the rest by advancing it up to 300 yards (275 m) in front to take all the enemy fire: The first wave kept the succeeding units relatively safe from enemy bullets. The speed of the attack depended on the distance to be covered. An attack was made at regulation quick time, a march of 110 steps per minute, which covered about 86 yards (78 m). In theory, lines struck the enemy positions in straight disciplined ranks, but in practice this was rarely accomplished.

New tactics

Tactics changed as the war went on. The tactics laid down in the manuals were out of date by 1861. The main reason for this was that the tactics were developed at a time when the infantryman's weapon was the smoothbore flintlock musket, which was inaccurate and had an effective range of only 60 yards (55 m). In the 1860s the introduction of rifled muskets

Curriculum Context

Students asked to discuss soldiers' experiences of battle might imagine how it felt to be involved in an infantry attack.

Flintlock

A firearm fired by a spark struck by a flint when the trigger is pulled.

Curriculum Context

Some curricula ask students to explain how changing technology impacted how the war was fought.

dramatically changed how battles were fought. The new rifled muskets could kill at 500 yards (450 m). Such weapons made the bayonet charge very dangerous and standing in line without cover a few hundred yards from the enemy an act of suicide.

Importance of using cover

Although charging in ranks in the face of enemy fire was dangerous, army commanders still believed such attacks could win battles. The Civil War was marked by a series of bloody and futile frontal assaults, such as the Union charges on Marye's Heights during the Battle of Fredericksburg in December 1862.

By 1864 soldiers were changing the way they were fighting as a result of bitter experience. Infantry attacks were now made in short rushes, with soldiers giving each other covering fire as they ran from one place of safety to another.

Curriculum Context

The next major conflict after the Civil War, World War I, was dominated by trench warfare.

Defensive trenches

In defense, getting out of the way of enemy fire became the first priority, and entrenchments were widely dug. As Union general Jacob D. Cox explained after the war, "One rifle in the trench was worth five in front of it." These were to become the new tactics that would dominate infantry warfare in the next 50 years.

The 96th Pennsylvania Infantry drilling at Camp Northumberland in 1861. Constant drilling was essential to deploy troops successfully on the battlefield.

Ironclads

The development during the Civil War of steam-powered armored warships, known as ironclads, had a great influence on naval warfare. Both sides spent a large amount of time and money developing this revolutionary type of vessel.

The Civil War hastened the development of these new ironclad warships, which formed a transitional phase between the old wooden sail-powered warships and the battleships of the late 19th century.

USS *Monitor*

In 1861 Union Secretary of the Navy Gideon Welles commissioned Swedish inventor John Ericsson to build the first Union ironclad. He completed his revolutionary ship, the USS *Monitor*, in January 1862. Some 172 feet (52 m) long and armed with two 11-inch (28-cm) Dahlgren guns in a revolving iron turret, the *Monitor* was technically the most advanced warship of its time. Its armor plating was 8 inches (20 cm) thick. Since it was almost impossible to make iron plates this thick, the armor of the *Monitor*, like most later ironclads, was made of 1-inch (2.5-cm) plates bolted together. The craft looked strange. It had a very low freeboard—the deck of the ship was only 1 foot (30 cm) above the waterline. Despite being barely seaworthy, the *Monitor* became the pattern for one of the most popular types of ironclad. Of the 52 coastal ironclads contracted for by the Union during the war, 48 followed this design.

> ### Curriculum Context
>
> Some curricula might ask you to give examples of the technological and industrial superiority of the Union during the war.

Casemate ironclads

The Union ordered 24 ironclads to patrol internal waters. Built with a casemate—an iron-plated box to protect the guns and crew—the first was launched in October 1861. Designed by Samuel M. Pook and known as "Pook Turtles," they contributed to Union victories on Western rivers in 1862 and 1863.

The Union casemate ironclad *Baron de Kalb* (formerly the *Saint Louis*). It was one of seven ironclads built for use on Western rivers that were known as "Pook Turtles" after their designer, Samuel M. Pook. The *Baron de Kalb* was sunk by a Confederate sea mine in the Yazoo River in 1863.

Curriculum Context

Students considering experiences on the Union home front could bear in mind the periodic fear of attack from the sea.

Curriculum Context

Victory in the war of the ironclads is another good example of the Union's many economic advantages over the South.

Confederate ironclads

The Confederacy lacked the facilities and resources to build large warships. It had only one major shipyard in New Orleans and one ironworks—Tredegar Ironworks in Richmond, Virginia. After Virginia seceded from the Union in 1861, Confederate forces took over the U.S. Navy's Norfolk shipyard and the U.S. Navy's new steamship, the *Merrimack*. Confederate engineers raised the partially destroyed *Merrimack* and built on its hull a large armored casemate. The name of its new casemate ironclad was the CSS *Virginia*, and it set sail in March 1862. The *Virginia* could operate both in coastal waters and on rivers. On March 9, 1862, the first ever battle between ironclads took place in Hampton Roads, Virginia, when the USS *Monitor* and CSS *Virginia* pounded each other for four-hours with no winner.

Ironclad-building programs

The appearance of the CSS *Virginia* briefly brought a fear that Confederate ironclads were about to attack Northern coastal cities. In the South women raised funds to build vessels, which were known as "Ladies' Gunboats." In the fall of 1862 the Confederacy began constructing a remarkable 18 ironclads.

On May 20, 1862, Union forces attacked the Norfolk shipyard to win it back. Confederates sank the *Virginia* to prevent it from falling into Union hands. This loss, along with the loss of four other ironclads and the fall of the ports of New Orleans and Memphis, proved that expectations of the new vessels had been too high. Enthusiasm in the South had waned by early 1863. In all, the Confederacy completed 22 ironclads during the war while the Union built more than 40. The Union's strengths in industry, skilled labor, and access to iron allowed it to outstrip the South in ironclad production.

Maps and Plans

Before the Civil War much of the United States was unmapped. Those maps that existed were often inaccurate or out of date. When war broke out in 1861, there was a desperate need to obtain reliable maps of the territory.

In order to plan the movements of their armies, Union and Confederate generals needed detailed information about terrain, river crossings, roads, and even houses, barns, and fences. During the Peninsular Campaign in Virginia in spring 1862 Union General George B. McClellan lamented that "correct local maps were not to be found … erroneous courses to streams and roads were frequently given." Both armies had trained mapmakers, known as topographical engineers, although the Union men had better surveying equipment. The Union also expanded the mapping work of the U.S. Coast Survey. In 1862 the Coast Survey printed 44,000 maps for military purposes: five times the number it produced in a typical prewar year.

When there was no time to have a map made, army topographers produced maps while accompanying troops on the move. At first maps were hand-traced onto thin linen to produce copies. Later, topographers also photographed maps to make copies more quickly. The copies were cut and mounted on cloth so they could be folded and fit in a pocket or saddlebag.

In enemy range

Civil War topographers often acted as reconnaissance officers as well as surveyors. They rode out a long way in front of the army to produce maps of the area ahead, and that brought them close to the enemy. They used that vantage point to make plans of the enemy's positions and fortifications, although working in sight and range of the opposing side was dangerous.

Curriculum Context

Many curricula expect students to understand the influence of geography on the progress of the war.

Topographers
Another name for map makers.

A few Civil War maps were sketched from balloons. Aeronaut John La Montain made one of the earliest such sketches on August 10, 1861, showing the location of Confederate tents and batteries at Sewall's Point, Virginia.

It was also the mapmaker's task to compile maps for battle reports. To do this, they had to liaise with divisional and corps officers after the battle to discover the exact positions of the different units during the fighting. We owe to their work much of our detailed knowledge of troop deployments in Civil War battles.

Jedediah Hotchkiss

One of the most successful topographers was a Confederate, Jedediah Hotchkiss. On March 26, 1862, he joined General Thomas "Stonewall" Jackson in the Shenandoah Valley. Jackson's description of his role was brief and to the point: "I want you to make me a map of the Valley, from Harpers Ferry to Lexington, showing all the points of offense and defense in those places." In the next three months Hotchkiss kept up a continual reconnaissance of the valley. He is credited with helping Jackson win the Valley Campaign (March–June 1862), in which Jackson's men covered 670 miles (1,070 km) and fought five battles. Hotchkiss continued to work with Jackson after the Valley Campaign. At the Battle of Chancellorsville in May 1863 he found a route for Jackson's corps through dense woods, which enabled Jackson to launch a surprise flank attack on the Union and win the battle.

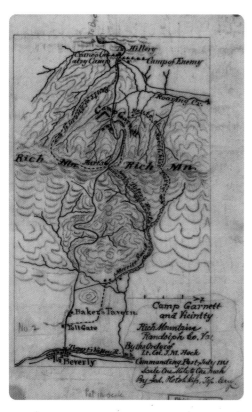

A map showing Union and Confederate positions at Rich Mountain, Virginia. The sketch map was made by Confederate topographer Jedediah Hotchkiss in July 1861.

Naval Warfare

The Civil War came at a time of great transition in naval warfare. As a result, technologically the war was characterized by novelty and experimentation. Ironclad vessels and sea mines (torpedoes) were widely used for the first time.

By 1861 steam power had largely supplanted sail as the chief means of moving a ship through water. Larger and more powerful cannons had been developed, while wooden warships, because of their vulnerability to improved shells, were giving way to ironclad vessels. The day of the sloop, frigate, and ship of the line were over, but naval architects had not yet worked out the best designs to replace them. Strategically, the tasks of both navies remained traditional. The Union navy had three objectives: to blockade the Confederacy's ports, to protect Union merchant ships on the high seas, and to take control of the South's coasts and navigable rivers, which could be used as invasion routes. The Confederate navy's strategy was essentially to prevent the Union from achieving its three aims.

Curriculum Context

Students might be asked to summarize Union naval strategy in the war.

The Union blockade

Before the war the United States had a modest navy of 90 warships, over half of which were in need of repair. With its substantial manufacturing capacity, the North soon began an impressive construction program supplemented by the purchase and conversion of numerous merchant vessels. By December 1864 the Union navy consisted of more than 600 ships, including 236 steam-powered vessels constructed during the war. Most of it went to enforce the Union blockade.

Merchant vessels

Unarmed ships used to carry commercial cargoes.

Effect of the blockade

The blockade greatly reduced the South's ability to market its only important export, cotton. Maintaining the blockade was a formidable task because the

Spar Torpedoes

The spar torpedo was an explosive placed at the end of a spar (long pole) and attached to the bow of a small boat. Manned by a crew of sailors, the spar torpedo boat rowed under cover of night until it got the torpedo next to the hull of an enemy vessel. The torpedo was attached to the spar by an iron slide, which could be detached from the boat. The torpedo would float up against the enemy vessel's hull and be exploded by pulling a separate lanyard (rope). With luck, the torpedo-boat crew would escape to safety, while the enemy vessel would be damaged or sunk.

A famous early attempt to use this technique was made by the CSS *Hunley*, a small submarine. In February 1864 the *Hunley* detonated its torpedo under the USS *Housatonic*. The attack succeeded, and the *Housatonic* became the first ship to be sunk by a submarine. But the *Hunley* was also dragged under by the suction of the vanishing *Housatonic*.

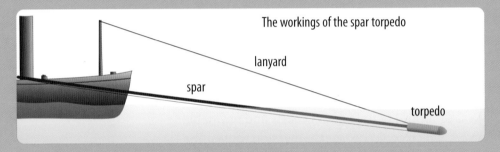

The workings of the spar torpedo

lanyard

spar

torpedo

Confederate states had a combined coastline of roughly 3,000 miles (4,830 km). Along this coast were hundreds of channels, rivers, and inlets. The Confederates used blockade-runners—steam-driven vessels designed for stealth and speed—to challenge the blockade. Although most succeeded, the Confederacy had relatively few blockade-runners. As a result, the cotton that left Southern ports was only a fraction of the amount shipped before the war.

Harbor defenses

The Union increased the effectiveness of the blockade by capturing Southern ports. The ports were defended by a combination of Confederate forts, ships, and sea mines, which were known as "torpedoes" in the Civil War. Some of the forts had been built before the war as

Curriculum Context

The Southern economy relied on cotton, so the inability to export the crop was a major blow to its economic strength.

part of the U.S. coastal defense system. Constructed mostly of thick masonry walls, they proved vulnerable to the new generation of large explosive shells. The Confederates soon discovered that earthen forts were easier to build and absorbed shell fire more effectively.

Confederate rams

The ships that defended Confederate harbors tended to be armored rams, which could sink an enemy vessel by ramming it as well as by firing on it with cannons. Both sides used rams in naval warfare, including some vessels that had no other armament, relying on their speed and iron ram to overcome the enemy.

The Confederacy constructed 22 rams. The most famous ironclad ram was the CSS *Virginia* (formerly the USS *Merrimack*), which during its brief existence protected Norfolk, Virginia. The most powerful Confederate ram was probably the CSS *Tennessee*, which helped guard the Alabama port of Mobile. The *Tennessee's* armor was 6 inches (15 cm) thick, and the vessel carried two 110-pounder and four 95-pounder cannons.

CSS *Virginia*
Learn more about the *Virginia* on page 56.

Torpedoes

Torpedoes were the third part of Confederate harbor defense. They did not move, and unlike modern sea mines, they did not explode on contact with a ship. (Reliable contact fuses had not yet been invented.) They were simply watertight cylinders packed with black powder (explosive) and submerged. A cable or other device kept the torpedo in place. Another cable ran to an observation post on shore. When an enemy ship came close to the mine, the shore observers detonated it using an electric current. Inefficient by later standards, the torpedo was the single most effective element in the Confederate naval arsenal. During the war torpedoes hit 29 Union warships—far more than were lost to ramming or gunfire.

Contact fuse
A fuse that detonated explosives when it was impacted by a hard surface, such as the hull of a ship.

Confederate guns of the stronghold of Port Hudson fire on Union warships on the Mississippi River. The battle for Port Hudson lasted almost four months. On July 8, 1863, Union forces finally captured it after a 47-day siege, gaining control of the whole of the Mississippi.

Commerce raiding

The South also built or bought from abroad several fast warships to raid Union maritime commerce, which the Confederacy manned with regular naval crews. Their job was to disrupt the Union's trade by destroying enemy merchant ships. The few Southern commerce raiders achieved great notoriety and in some respects great effectiveness. They sank a large number of Union merchant ships and forced hundreds more to seek refuge by reregistering under neutral flags—a blow from which the American maritime trade never fully recovered. The greatest of them was the CSS *Alabama*, commanded by Raphael Semmes, which took 64 prizes worth more than $6.5 million. The *Alabama* was finally cornered and sunk by the USS *Kearsarge* outside the port of Cherbourg, France, in June 1864.

Seizing Confederate rivers and coasts

The Union built nearly 60 ironclad vessels. Naval engineers tried out different designs, notably the USS *New Ironsides,* with 16 11-inch Dahlgren guns. The *New Ironsides* had one major difference: the 4½-inch (11-cm) thick belt of armor that protected most of its hull. Launched in May 1862, *New Ironsides* served through the war, notably in the prolonged but unsuccessful attempt in 1863 to capture Charleston, South Carolina.

The most famous Union ironclad was the USS *Monitor*, launched in January 1862. It fought the world's first duel between armored warships in a famous engagement with the CSS *Virginia*, on March 9, 1862, at Hampton Roads, Virginia. The *Monitor*'s key feature, an armored turret capable of turning its two guns in any direction, became in modified form a standard design for all future warships. However, the *Monitor* proved to have one drawback: Its low hull could not handle heavy seas, so it was unsuitable for coastal use. It foundered in a storm and sank less than a year after it was launched. It was, however, a good design for a naval war fought in protected coastal waters.

Triumph of the ironclads

Naval observers across the world understood the significance of the ironclad duel. As the *Times* newspaper in London noted, Britain's Royal Navy had gone from having 149 first-class warships to having exactly two: its twin experimental ironclads.

Without the Union navy the Union army might well not have been able to subdue the Confederacy. Only control of the seas and rivers cut off the Confederacy from the world and enabled the Union armies to be transported deep into the Confederacy.

Curriculum Context

You might be asked to assess how much the naval war contributed to the course of the overall conflict.

River Gunboats

While ironclads fought for possession of Confederate harbors, other new types of warships fought for possession of Confederate-held rivers. This was a war of small vessels mounting a few cannons. A few had light iron armor and were known as "tinclads," but many were protected by "armor" made from cotton bales. The armor had to be light so that the vessels did not draw too much water to navigate up shallow rivers and inlets. Although the Confederates constructed a few gunboats, they relied mainly on shore-based artillery to guard their navigable rivers.

The North, by contrast, built or converted dozens of gunboats. They played a vital role in the war in the western theater. Union gunboats assisted in the capture of Forts Henry and Donelson in February 1862, then exploited these victories by raiding far up the Tennessee and Cumberland rivers, which the forts had been built to defend. They were crucial to the Union army's campaign against Vicksburg, Mississippi, in 1863, for they protected the transports that Union General Ulysses S. Grant's troops needed to launch the campaign and supply it once it had begun.

Northern Virginia, Army of

Commanded for the entire three years of its existence by Robert E. Lee, the Confederate Army of Northern Virginia had a record of long marches, dramatic battles, and victories that earned it an impressive reputation.

The Army of Northern Virginia's reputation resulted in it becoming the embodiment of the Confederacy. When General Joseph E. Johnston, the commander of the Confederacy's eastern army, was wounded at Fair Oaks, Virginia, on May 31, 1862, President Jefferson Davis replaced him with Robert E. Lee. Taking command on June 1, Lee renamed his force of around 70,000 men the Army of Northern Virginia.

On the offensive

Within a month of taking command Lee was ready to go on the offensive, a mode of warfare for which he would become famous. In the Seven Days' Campaign, a series of frequently uncoordinated and bloody attacks, Lee's army drove the Union Army of the Potomac away from Richmond, the Confederate capital.

Lee then embarked on a series of battles that saw the army march northward through Virginia, winning victories at Cedar Mountain and Second Bull Run (Manassas), and into Maryland. There its depleted ranks suffered a tactical draw at Antietam in September 1862, and Lee was forced to withdraw into Virginia. He reorganized his army into a two-corps structure, with Generals Thomas J. "Stonewall" Jackson and James Longstreet as his corps commanders. Further stunning victories followed at Fredericksburg (December 1862) and Chancellorsville (May 1863), confirming the army's status as the most successful Confederate force despite the death of "Stonewall" Jackson at Chancellorsville, where he was accidentally shot by Confederates.

Curriculum Context

Many curricula ask students to appreciate the role in the war of significant individuals: Robert E. Lee was one of the most influential of all commanders in the war.

Curriculum Context

If you are asked to describe turning points in the war, Antietam may well be included.

Second reorganization

Following his loss, Lee reorganized the army again, this time into three army corps, commanded initially by Longstreet, Richard S. Ewell, and Ambrose P. Hill. This 75,000 strong army marched into Pennsylvania, where it suffered its most important defeat at Gettysburg in early July 1863. The damage done was irreparable. An estimated 23,000 casualties, including heavy losses among the officer corps, robbed Lee's army of its offensive striking power. From then on Lee had to fight on the defensive, reacting to his enemy's moves.

Curriculum Context

The Confederate defeat at Gettysburg is often identified as the turning point of the whole war.

The end comes

When General Ulysses S. Grant came east in early 1864 he made his headquarters with the Union Army of the Potomac, a recognition that he regarded Lee's army as his most dangerous opponent. The Overland Campaign left the exhausted armies within sight of Richmond and Lee's legions shattered by more than 30,000 casualties, including 37 general officers. The ten-month siege at Petersburg saw Lee's reduced forces hold out until early April 1865, when successive offensives by Grant's army forced Lee to evacuate the city. Lee was unable to escape. Grant surrounded Lee's small band at Appomattox Court House, Virginia. On April 9, 1865, Lee surrendered 28,000 men of his once-mighty army. The Army of Northern Virginia was beaten, but had earned an enviable place in military history.

Robert E. Lee with his officers at Fredericksburg, the scene of one of the Army of Northern Virginia's greatest triumphs.

Potomac, Army of the

Created in August 1861, the Army of the Potomac was the Union's main field force in the eastern theater. It was also usually the Union's largest army at any given time, with an average strength of about 120,000 men.

The Army of the Potomac was a hard-luck outfit. In four years of combat it lost almost every major battle it fought. The army had two principal missions. Offensively, its job was to threaten the Confederate capital of Richmond, Virginia, and, in the process, to destroy the rival army. Defensively, its job was to shield Washington, D.C. Often the latter task hampered efforts to accomplish the first. The proximity of the army to the Union capital meant that politics exerted a heavy and largely negative influence over its operations.

First commander

The army's first commander was also its creator, General George B. McClellan. The Army of the Potomac kept the stamp of his personality throughout the war. McClellan was cautious, systematic, politically conservative, and suspicious of Abraham Lincoln's administration. In combat he overestimated the enemy's resourcefulness and strength. McClellan's subordinates acquired and emulated these characteristics and reflected them in every campaign.

A story from the Battle of the Wilderness (May 5–6, 1864) illustrates the problem. A report reached the army on the second evening that Robert E. Lee's army had launched a flank attack. General Ulysses S. Grant, traveling with the Army of the Potomac, was approached by a flustered officer. Fed up with hearing defeatist talk, Grant snapped, "Go back to your command, and try to think what we are going to do ourselves, instead of what Lee is going to do."

Curriculum Context

McClellan's influence should be included in discussions of the Union conduct of the war.

Injured soldiers leave the fierce fighting on the battlefield of Gettysburg (July 1–3, 1863). The Army of the Potomac's victory at Gettysburg was a turning point in the war, bringing a string of Confederate victories to an end.

Defensiveness remained typical of the army. However, its troops fought bravely in some of the bloodiest and most famous battles of the war, including the Seven Days' Campaign, Antietam, Fredericksburg, Chancellorsville, Gettysburg, the Overland Campaign, and the Siege of Petersburg.

Four generals commanded the army. They were McClellan (August 20, 1861–November 9, 1862), Ambrose E. Burnside (November 9, 1862–January 26, 1863), Joseph Hooker (January 26–June 28, 1863), and George G. Meade (June 28, 1863 –September 1, 1865). Ulysses S. Grant, who became commander of all Union armies in March 1864, made his headquarters with the army and gave detailed instructions to Meade. But even Grant could not break the army of its overcaution.

Greatest moments

The Army of the Potomac had three great moments. The first was on July 1–3, 1863, when it rebuffed Lee's invasion of Pennsylvania at the Battle of Gettysburg. The second came on April 1, 1865, when it opened the flank of Lee's army defending the Petersburg trenches in the Battle of Five Forks. This set the stage for Lee's retreat. The Army of the Potomac pursued, and eight days later it enjoyed a third great moment by forcing Lee's surrender at Appomattox Court House on April 9.

Curriculum Context

Ulysses S. Grant was one of the greatest Union commanders of the war.

Curriculum Context

All three of the army's great moments deserve to be included in a list of turning points of the war.

Prisoner-of-War Camps

More than 400,000 soldiers are believed to have been held prisoner during the Civil War. In the prisoner-of-war camps, more than 30,000 Union men and 25,000 Confederates died from starvation or disease.

For much of the war the policy of both sides was not to keep prisoners but to release them on parole—prisoners had to promise not to take up arms again until exchanged for an enemy soldier. The first prisoner exchange took place in February 1862. In July both sides agreed to parole prisoners within 10 days and to exchange them at an agreed rate. One general could be exchanged for 60 enlisted men. But by the summer of 1863 the exchange system had broken down due to a lack of trust on both sides. By late 1864 the number of prisoners being held in camps had soared into the hundreds of thousands. Conditions were dreadful.

Curriculum Context

What factors might contribute to a breakdown of trust over prisoner exchanges?

The first prisons
At the beginning of the war prisoners waiting to be paroled were held in coastal forts. The Confederacy held prisoners taken at Bull Run (Manassas) at Castle Pinckney in Charleston, and the Union used Fort Warren in Boston Harbor.

The Union founded a purpose-built prison camp for Confederate officers on Johnson's Island in Lake Erie off Ohio in June 1862. In the South the system of housing prisoners was less organized and suffered from a lack of resources. There was no money to build new prisons, so warehouses were used, like Libby Prison in Richmond. Men were locked inside and left with guards outside. As in most Civil War prisons there was no privacy, no comfort, and no sanitation. In one room more than 200 prisoners were crammed into a space measuring only 30 feet (9 m) by 70 feet (21 m).

Curriculum Context

The experience of prisoners of war is often overlooked in discussions of what the war was like for the men who fought in it.

Crisis point

In March 1864 Union General Ulysses S. Grant stopped prisoner exchanges, accusing Confederates of sending troops back into action who had given their parole not to fight. The Confederates had also threatened to treat captured black troops as escaped slaves and not prisoners of war.

As prisoner numbers rose, both the Union and Confederacy resorted to using vast open-air enclosures to hold them. The Union War Department opened the notorious Elmira Prison in New York State in May 1864. By August it was filled with 10,000 Confederates, half of them living in tents on a badly drained, polluted swamp. By November more than 700 men had died from typhoid, dysentery, pneumonia, or smallpox, and 1,000 men a day were falling sick. Some died from scurvy due to a lack of fresh vegetables in their rations.

Andersonville

In February 1864 the Confederates opened Camp Sumter near Andersonville in Georgia. The camp was meant to relieve the pressure on prisons around Richmond, but men were sent there without any regard to conditions or how they might be fed. By July more than 32,000 men were crowded into the camp without any shelter from the sun and on starvation rations. The terrible conditions suffered by Union prisoners at Andersonville were first publicized in the North in late 1864, when a pamphlet published in

Black troops
You can learn more about black troops on pages 10–13.

Scurvy
A disease caused by the lack of Vitamin C.

A drawing by Alfred Waud shows returned Union prisoners of war obtaining new clothing on board the USS *New York* in December 1864.

Boston recorded the experiences of prisoners who had survived there. Daily rations at Andersonville were 2 ounces of pork (56 g), usually half rotting, plus a little rice and corn bread. Prisoners lacked wood for a cooking fire or a pan to cook in. Starvation, sickness, and depression were rife, and many prisoners either lay motionless or stalked vacantly up and down.

Death toll

By August 1864 there were 35,000 men in Andersonville, and the death toll from starvation and disease had climbed to 100 a day. By April 1865 the total number of deaths in the camp had reached 13,000, although this may be an underestimate. There were calls in the North for retribution against the Confederate officers responsible. Immediately after the war ended, the camp commandant, Henry Wirz, was tried by a U.S. military tribunal, charged with cruelty and conspiracy to kill Union prisoners of war. He was found guilty and hanged in late 1865.

Military tribunal
A military court.

Conditions at Andersonville

This is part of the testimony of Private Prescott Tracy, of the 82nd New York, who was captured during the Siege of Petersburg in June 1864 and held in Andersonville.

"On entering the Stockade Prison, we found it crowded with 28,000 of our fellow soldiers. By crowded, I mean that it was difficult to move in any direction without jostling or being jostled. This prison is an open space without trees or shelter of any kind. . . . Through the ground . . . runs or rather creeps a stream through an artificial channel, varying from five to six feet in width, the water about ankle deep, and near the middle of the enclosure, spreading out into a swamp of about six acres, filled with refuse. . . . The water is of a dark color and an ordinary glass would collect a thick sediment. This is our only drinking and cooking water.

"Our only shelter from the sun and rain and night dews was what we could make by stretching over us our coats or scraps of blankets, which a few of us had, but generally there was no attempt by day or night to protect ourselves. The clothing of the men was miserable in the extreme. Very few had shoes of any kind, not two thousand had coats and pants, and those were latecomers. More than one-half were indecently exposed, and many were naked."

Reconnaissance

The fundamental role of reconnaissance is to tell an army commander where the enemy is, what he is doing, and what the surrounding area is like. In the Civil War, which was often fought on unmapped terrain, reconnaissance was crucial.

Much of the countryside over which the armies marched and fought was semiwilderness that only local people knew well enough to travel through without getting lost. For a lot of the time armies were moving almost blindly through unknown country as they tried to find and fight the enemy.

Chancellorsville

Some of the most famous battles involved failures of reconnaissance. The Battle of Shiloh, which began on April 6, 1862, started with a surprise attack by 9,000 Confederates on the camps of General Ulysses S. Grant's troops. The Union troops had no idea that an entire Confederate army was advancing to attack.

The Confederates surprised the Union forces a second time at the Battle of Chancellorsville in Virginia on May 2, 1863, when Confederate General Robert E. Lee sent Thomas J. "Stonewall" Jackson and 28,000 men on a flanking march to attack the Union right flank. In a brilliant piece of reconnaissance work the whole force—almost two-thirds of Lee's army—found its way through 12 miles (19 km) of forest. In the late afternoon Jackson launched his attack, taking the Union army's XI Corps completely by surprise. Only nightfall saved the Union troops from defeat.

The role of cavalry

The soldiers most heavily involved in reconnaissance work were cavalrymen. Armies relied on riders to scout forward of the main army to seek out the enemy, sometimes with the help of local guides or spies. During the Peninsular Campaign in June 1862, J.E.B. Stuart led a Confederate force of 1,200 men in a reconnaissance around Union General George B. McClellan's army. Stuart's ride took three days and told Lee exactly where the Union army was. The information was to prove vital 10 days later, when Lee began a counterattack in the first of what would become known as the Seven Days' Battles.

Curriculum Context

The Union victory in the turning-point battle at Gettysburg directly links successful reconnaissance with the ultimate outcome of the whole conflict.

Army commanders depended on the reconnaissance work of the cavalry. One of the reasons often given for the Union victory at Gettysburg in July 1863 is that the Union cavalry reached the battlefield first and took up a good defensive position on Cemetery Hill. Likewise, one of the explanations given for the Confederate defeat is that Stuart's cavalry failed to reconnoiter in front of Lee's army, so the general had no way of knowing that General George G. Meade was concentrating the whole of the Army of the Potomac on the high ground above Gettysburg.

Infantry soldiers also carried out reconnaissance on the battlefield. The tactics involved pushing out companies of troops up to 500 yards (460 m) in front of the main battle line to act as skirmishers. Acting independently or in small groups, the men gave advance warning of an oncoming attack. This was important, since the gunpowder created clouds of thick smoke that in fierce firefights cut visibility down to a few hundred feet.

Signalers

Learn more about communications and signals on pages 19–22.

Signalers and reconnaissance

Signalers had an important role. Once the enemy was found, it was important to get information back quickly to the commanding generals. Increasingly men of the signal corps could be found on the front line, risking their lives to send back information on enemy movements using a semaphore system of flags, colored lights, or signal flares.

River War

The South was dissected by thousands of miles of rivers, and control of these waterways was to be the key to Union victory. Throughout the war the Union navy fought for supremacy over these vital river links.

The Union navy had an ever-growing fleet of wooden sailing ships and steamships, plus a new technology: the ironclad gunboat. With them it could attack and overwhelm Confederate river defenses. Once the rivers were secured the Union could use them to move its troops and supplies long distances. The fledgling Confederate navy, suffering from shortages of men and materials, could not match its Union counterpart.

The river war in the west occurred roughly in three phases. The first, from January to March 1862, saw Union forces concentrate on the Tennessee and Cumberland rivers. Commodore Andrew Foote and General Ulysses S. Grant carried out a model campaign of joint army–navy operations, capturing Forts Henry and Donelson, and opening up the Tennessee and Cumberland rivers all the way to Corinth, Mississippi and Florence, Alabama.

Phase two of the western naval campaign, from March 1862 to July 1863, attempted to open the length of the Mississippi River as a line of communication for Union forces. Foote and John Pope operated against Confederate forts north of Memphis, Tennessee, in 1862, completing the capture of most of Tennessee for Union forces. Grant, Foote, and David D. Porter cooperated in 1863 to besiege Vicksburg, Mississippi, which fell on July 4, 1863. With Vicksburg in Union hands, the last fort on the Mississippi—Port Hudson—surrendered, and Union naval forces had free access to the entire length of the river.

Curriculum Context

Few major wars have depended on control of waterways as much as the Civil War, so riverboat technology was of unique importance to the progress of the conflict.

Curriculum Context

The Union's winning of control of the whole Mississippi was one of the decisive moments of the war.

Red River Campaign

Phase three of the western campaign, the 1864 Red River expedition, was the least successful. Falling water levels in the Red River almost stranded Porter's gunboat fleet at Alexandria, but thanks to 3,000 Union soldiers who hastily built dams to retain the water, it managed to escape just in time.

River war in the east

The York and James rivers were crucial in General George McClellan's 1862 Peninsular Campaign. He moved his entire army via Chesapeake Bay to Fortress Monroe, Virginia. He then used river transports and gunboats to establish a supply depot at White House Landing on the Pamunkey River, only 20 miles (32 km) from the Confederate capital, Richmond.

Natural defenses

Rivers created a major obstacle for the Union armies in Virginia. Most of the rivers in the state run west to east, while the Union armies generally advanced north to south (apart from the Peninsular Campaign). Any Union force had to contend with a series of rivers, which formed a natural defensive line for the Confederates.

Transports
Ships for carrying military equipment or supplies.

Union ships landing supplies on the James River during the Petersburg Campaign. Vital supplies brought in by river enabled the Union forces to besiege Petersburg for 10 months.

Sharpshooters

Both the Union and the Confederacy employed units of highly trained marksmen, known as sharpshooters, who performed a front-line role. They demoralized the enemy by the accuracy of their shooting, often targeting senior officers.

Sharpshooters played a vital role in the Civil War. The fear of their expert marksmanship had a strong psychological effect on their enemies. They were organized into special units that could operate independently of large units, performing scouting and skirmishing duties.

Berdan's Sharpshooters

At the outbreak of war both Union and Confederate armies formed special sharpshooter battalions and regiments. The most famous was the 1st U.S. Sharpshooters, formed by New Yorker Hiram Berdan in November 1861. Recruits had to pass a difficult shooting test in which they had to fire 10 bullets into a 10-inch (25-cm) circle 200 yards (180 m) away. Berdan's Sharpshooters took part in all the campaigns of the Army of the Potomac, exhibiting both bravery and skill.

In July 1862 the Confederate Congress authorized the formation of sharpshooter battalions within standard infantry brigades. Brigade commanders could handpick men from each regiment for this demanding and risky duty. Because of the extra training involved, they were often exempted from standard camp duties; in combat they served as advance and rear guards on the march and as skirmishers once fighting began. Confederate sharpshooters had to be able to hit a man-sized target at 600 yards (550 m). Sharpshooters in both armies were usually equipped with specialized rifles, frequently with telescopic sights.

Curriculum Context

The role of sharpshooters was to undermine the enemy's morale, rather than to have any real effect on its physical strength.

Curriculum Context

Telescopic sights are an example of technological innovation during the war that encouraged the development of new forms of fighting, such as the use of sharpshooters.

Siege Warfare

At the time of the Civil War, capturing fortifications and cities by siege was considered to be one of the most precise military arts. The armies of the 1860s followed a method of attack perfected in Europe over the previous 200 years.

Curriculum Context

Many primary sources such as diaries and newspaper reports recorded living conditions for those in the besieged cities.

Shot

Cannisters packed with smaller pellets or balls that spray out on firing.

Siege warfare went through various stages and was a slow and destructive business. The first move was to "invest" the enemy position, which meant surrounding it and cutting off all routes of escape or resupply. This was sometimes enough to end a siege before it began because it presented the enemy with the starkest of choices—surrender or face slow starvation.

The next step was to position the siege artillery. Bigger and heavier than field artillery, weighing up to 5,000 lb (2,260 kg), they were maneuverable enough to be transported on wheeled carriages. They could fire 32-lb (14.5-kg) shot or shells and had a range of up to 2,000 yards (1,828 m). During the Siege of Vicksburg, Mississippi, Union General Ulysses S. Grant had over 220 guns pounding the city. He also used the most feared piece of artillery, the mortar. Developed specifically for sieges, this short, squat weapon could fire shells in a high arc straight over enemy defenses to land inside the fort or city. There was no defense against mortar fire. The mortars Grant used at Vicksburg were huge, some with barrels as wide as 13 inches (33 cm) that were powerful enough to fire shells over the Mississippi River and hit Vicksburg on the opposite bank.

With the arrival of the guns, the siege became an artillery duel. The attacking side looked for weaknesses in the enemy defenses, while the besieged garrison moved its artillery around to meet the next expected assault with as much firepower as it could muster.

Digging trenches

A siege could not be won by artillery alone. As the bombardment continued, the besieging infantry would be digging entrenchments closer and closer to the enemy's forward defenses in preparation for the opening of a breach into which an assault could be made. First a ring of trenches, known as a parallel, was dug; then trenches were dug forward of them and linked with a second parallel. Digging was slow, hard work and went on day and night under constant fire from snipers and enemy artillery. In order to defend themselves, the men worked behind a sap-roller, a device one Illinois soldier at Vicksburg described as a "bullet stopper." It was a large basket made of woven saplings filled with earth. Pushing it ahead of them, the soldiers digging the trenches could keep working in comparative safety.

Using explosives

A breach could also be made by digging a tunnel under the defenders' positions, filling it with gunpowder, and blowing it up. The Union army used this method twice, at Vicksburg in June 1863 and 13 months later in July 1864 at the Siege of Petersburg,

Snipers

Expert marksmen whose task was to target and kill individuals on the enemy side.

A Union battery of immense 13-inch (33-cm) mortars lined up at the Siege of Yorktown, Virginia, in April 1862. Mortars were used to pound away at the earthworks and fortifications around towns and forts.

Virginia. On both occasions the explosives blew a huge gap in the Confederate defenses, but the Union infantry that charged into the breach could not climb out of the crater created by the explosion. Instead of taking advantage of the artillery bombardment, they became a sitting target for the Confederate defenders, who quickly reorganized themselves after the initial shock. The attack at Petersburg was particularly bloody. The Union army lost 4,000 men in what became known as the Battle of the Crater.

The Confederates were not powerless against Union siege tactics. To defend themselves from Union army tunnels, the Southerners used the old defense of digging a countermine—a tunnel deliberately dug under the Union tunnel, which could then be collapsed or blown up. There were also more modern innovations such as hand grenades, which the Confederates used at Vicksburg, together with improvised weapons including artillery shells with lighted fuses that were rolled down breastworks toward the attackers. Both proved very effective in close-quarter fighting on the front lines.

Lack of supplies

For all the bloodshed sieges caused, most of them ended not with a final assault of attacking infantry but with the surrender of the defenders, driven out of their fortifications by hunger. The Confederates trapped inside Vicksburg were eating mule and rat meat by the time they surrendered to Grant on July 4, 1863. About 150 miles (240 km) to the south Confederates at Port Hudson, Louisiana, the last Southern post on the Mississippi River, held out for 47 days before finally surrendering. From late May the garrison fought off a Union army of more than 30,000 until starvation, disease, and the news of the fall of Vicksburg led the city's commander, General Franklin Gardner, to surrender on July 8, 1863.

Curriculum Context

Students studying innovations in siege technology should also consider developments in defending against sieges.

A drawing by Alfred Waud of Union cannons firing on Confederate positions during the Siege of Petersburg, Virginia, the longest siege in North American history. Confederate General Robert E. Lee's army held off Union General Ulysses S. Grant's forces for 10 months in 1864–1865.

The last siege

The siege of Petersburg ended in April 1865 because General Robert E. Lee had to break out from his trench lines to secure access to his only source of resupply, the railroad line to the west. Lee's army had built a massive trench system around the city that from June 1864 had successfully kept Grant and the Army of the Potomac at bay. But the siege had lasted 10 months, and Lee knew his army could only grow weaker as Grant's grew stronger. A fresh Union offensive would certainly see the Confederate army destroyed, so Lee ordered his men to evacuate Petersburg and led them westward toward the rail station near Appomattox, where he was forced to surrender on April 9.

Defending territory with fortifications was one of the Confederacy's main strategies, particularly in the western theater. In the end it proved to be a weakness. The South was fighting a defensive war, relying on fortified positions to defend territory it claimed was no longer part of the United States because it did not have the huge armies needed to cover such a vast area. This strategy had two drawbacks. No matter how strong the fortifications were or how difficult the terrain, the Union army had the resources and manpower to find a way through and attack. It took a year of fighting down the Mississippi River before Grant was able to lay siege to Vicksburg. By defending these positions, the Confederacy tied down thousands of men in sieges they could not win instead of using them in field armies that had a far better chance of an even fight.

Curriculum Context

Students might be asked to evaluate the Confederates' defensive strategy and its strengths and weaknesses.

Soldier Life

The citizen-soldiers of the Civil War endured remarkable hardships during their time in service. But through it all these men maintained a sense of humor and faced fear, deprivation, disease, and death with impressive courage.

Curriculum Context

It is important to understand the background of most soldiers to appreciate their experiences during the war.

The average Civil War soldier was white, Protestant, and young—usually between 18 and 29 years old. Most of them came from relatively isolated rural areas. Before the war required them to march across the country, most soldiers had never been farther than a few miles from their homes. These men enlisted out of a very basic form of patriotism—the belief that their way of life was under attack. Peer pressure and friendships were also often factors in the decision to enlist.

The thousands of new recruits found their first exposure to army life unsettling. Many young men had never been away from home before and suffered from homesickness. Unfamiliar living conditions, combined with the novelties of military life, led to an outpouring of letters and diaries that remains unmatched in American history.

Citizen-soldiers

Turning thousands of farmers, shopkeepers, and laborers into soldiers was an arduous task. It usually began in "camps of instruction," often located in or near state capitals, where newly formed regiments received their initial training. Most officers on both sides had little or no military training, meaning that the men responsible for training new soldiers were learning their duties as they went along. Both armies tried to fill their officer ranks with men educated at military academies or with militia experience, but the size of the armies meant thousands of Civil War officers were as inexperienced as the men they led.

Militia

Bodies of armed civilians trained to fight in times of emergency.

Drill and more drill

Aside from combat, the dominant fact of life for the Civil War soldier was drill. Training consisted primarily of drill—learning first how to handle and fire weapons, and then the individual and unit movements necessary to cover ground, maneuver on the battlefield, and deliver a heavy volume of fire at the enemy. Having to learn drill movements taught the soldiers discipline and unit cohesion. One Union soldier wrote in a letter home, "The first thing in the morning is drill, then drill, then drill again. Then drill, drill, a little more drill. Then drill, and lastly drill. Between drills, we drill and sometimes stop to eat a little and have roll-call."

Between bouts of drill the soldiers carried out various forms of manual labor, known as "fatigues." They included digging latrines, cleaning the camp, foraging for wood for heating and cooking, and carrying water from the nearest stream. Soldiers also organized their own amusements in the form of team games, songfests, and (although strictly forbidden) gambling. Enlisted men were prohibited from purchasing alcohol, but drinking was nevertheless prevalent. Men smuggled alcohol into camp or even made it themselves. One recipe called for "bark juice, tar-water, turpentine, brown sugar, and lamp oil."

Curriculum Context

Drill aimed to make soldiers' movements automatic, so they could perform them under fire almost automatically.

Gambling

It was not unknown for soldiers to lose an entire month's pay on the journey back from the paymaster to their tent.

Raw Officers

Volunteer officers had an extraordinarily difficult time learning how to drill their men and at the same time earn their respect and confidence. One artilleryman commented, "Maneuvers of the most utterly impossible sort were taught to the men. Every amateur officer had his own pet system of tactics, and the effect of the incongruous teachings, when brought out in battalion drill, closely resembled that of the music at Mr. Bob Sawyer's party, where each guest sang the chorus to the tune he knew best." Officers and sergeants usually studied among themselves at night, reciting and memorizing drill manuals and army regulations. As the weeks turned to months throughout 1861, civilians gradually became soldiers and prepared for combat.

Tarnished glory

Over time, battles, campaigns, long marches, and rough conditions took their toll, and dreams of glory and novelty of military life wore off. Poor food often led to disease. A boring diet of fried or salted meat, hard bread or crackers, and coffee, which was only rarely supplemented by fresh fruits and vegetables, reduced resistance to disease and laid the soldier open to diarrhea, dysentery, and chronic malnutrition. Soldiers on both sides noted they were frequently hungry, a condition that eventually lowered morale and reduced combat effectiveness.

Unsanitary camp conditions and year-round exposure to the elements laid thousands of soldiers low with malaria, cholera, measles, and pneumonia. Large groups of men, packed closely together in muddy camps, eating bad food and drinking tainted water, were perfect breeding grounds for disease.

Preparing for combat

Even though most of a Civil War soldier's life was spent in camp or on the march, combat was still the defining experience of his existence. "Seeing the elephant," as many referred to combat, offered moments of terror that punctuated the routine boredom of a soldier's life. Civil War battles and campaigns generally began in camp, with an order to prepare several days' rations and to be ready to march the next day. Excitement usually gave way to boredom and fatigue on the march, as heat and dust took their toll on men

Troops train outside Washington, D.C. The soldiers practice maneuvers in front of the "camp of instruction" on top of the hill.

The Strain of Combat

Paintings of Civil War battles often show orderly lines of men charging and defending as if on parade. In reality, every soldier fought his own battle, both against the enemy and against his own fears. Smoke, noise, and confusion reduced orderly lines of battle to chaos. The fear of showing cowardice was much stronger than any fear of death or wounds; this helps explain the often suicidal bravery of the Civil War soldier. Sustained combat produced a variety of emotions, from paralyzing fear to superhuman courage. Men under fire often went "berserk," loading and firing, charging and retreating with their comrades, in a frenzy of activity as time seemed to stand still.

tramping along unimproved roads. At the battlefield, officers and sergeants formed columns of marching men into lines of battle, a process that could take several hours. Leaders often gave their troops prebattle "pep talks" reminding the men of their commitments to home and country, of the glory of their cause, and of the difficult task ahead of them.

On the battlefield

After this, lines of battle lurched into the unknown. If a unit was within range of the enemy's artillery, but not within rifle range, the next few minutes could be highly demoralizing: being forced to march in the open with no opportunity to strike back at the enemy, and with his comrades falling around him as he marched. When units took their places in a larger line of battle for an attack, commanders straightened the ranks and issued orders to move forward against the enemy's line of battle.

The job of a unit on the attack was to maneuver to within range of the enemy, deliver massed rifle fire into their ranks to scatter the defenders, and then to charge to destroy the enemy's line or to occupy a piece of ground. A unit on the defense had to stand its ground and deliver as high a volume of fire as possible at an attacking enemy.

Glory

Military theory suggests that soldiers are more motivated to fight for their companions than for an abstract cause.

Curriculum Context

The drill that soldiers complained about ultimately enabled them to deliver the required massed fire on the battlefield.

Union infantry lined up waiting to advance on Confederate positions outside Petersburg. Officers tried to keep battle formation in the face of enemy fire.

Field hospitals

Civil War surgery was a gruesome business, made difficult by a general lack of understanding of disease and infection, and by a lack of surgical equipment to deal with the appalling wounds produced by the weapons of the day. Rifle balls, together with canister and shell fragments, produced jagged wounds that were difficult to treat under the best of circumstances. Amputating a wounded arm or leg was often the only available course of action; stories abounded of piles of amputated limbs outside field hospitals on both sides. The rudimentary anesthetics of the day did little to ease the patient's pain during this process. However, surgeons were generally well qualified for their work and, despite their reputations as butchers, labored heroically under difficult conditions.

Religion and comradeship

Religion was an important part of everyday life in 19th-century America, and many soldiers took a strong faith into the army. Religious services and prayer meetings offered a way to make sense of the horrors of combat and the boredom of camp life. Men of both sides saw their military duty as an aspect of their faith giving meaning to their experience. Victory in battle was a gift from God; defeat was punishment for a transgression. Religious revivals regularly swept through both armies, supplementing the regular schedule of church services.

Drill, fatigue, boredom, fear, disease, death—these constant companions made a Civil War soldier's life a difficult one. However, the average soldier endured these hardships with resignation and humor, and did his job with bravery and skill.

Curriculum Context

If curricula ask you to describe soldiers' experience in the war, the role of religion could be something to consider.

Strategy and Tactics

Both the Union and Confederacy used a variety of strategies to try and achieve their war objectives. They involved not only military operations but diplomatic, political, and economic strategies and tactics as well.

Strategy is the art of planning and directing large military operations and movements, often to obtain a specific objective. Tactics is the art of disposing military forces for battle and maneuvering them on the battlefield. Both terms can be used in a nonmilitary sense to describe any method or series of maneuvers used to gain advantage or success. In war military strategy is usually part of a broader strategy that includes politics, economics, and diplomacy.

Both sides used the diplomatic tactics of propaganda, personal relationships, and economic pressure to enlist the support of the European powers and even Mexico. The Confederacy, hoping to obtain recognition as an independent nation and to obtain financial or military aid from Britain and France, sent its own representatives to these three nations, where the Union government already had representatives.

The Anaconda Plan

The North used diplomatic means to enlist support for its cause and prevent the Confederacy being given independent nation status. Diplomacy was followed by a naval strategy, General-in-Chief Winfield Scott's "Anaconda Plan." Scott proposed a naval blockade of Southern ports to stop the South from importing the war supplies it needed and also to stop the export of cotton. The strategy was not popular because there was too much enthusiasm in the North to go to the fight, although elements of the plan were put in place, such as the naval blockade of Southern ports.

> **Diplomacy**
> The practice of maintaining relations between countries.

> **Curriculum Context**
> The "Anaconda Plan"—named for the snake that squeezes its victims to death—is an important element in the early part of the war.

A cartoon illustrating the 1861 strategy proposed by Union General Winfield Scott to defeat the South. By blockading Southern ports and gaining control of the major rivers, Scott hoped to win the war without bloodshed by strangling the South economically. It was called the "Anaconda Plan" after the large snake that squeezes its prey to death.

Cotton diplomacy

The Confederacy did not have a navy powerful enough to break a blockade. Instead, it followed a strategy of "cotton diplomacy." Confederate President Jefferson Davis encouraged planters to withhold cotton, believing that at the "first wail from England's manufacturing districts" British and French fleets would arrive and end the blockade. The strategy failed—the Confederacy overestimated Britain and France's dependency on Southern cotton. Lincoln got the upper hand in the diplomatic war when in 1863 he issued the Emancipation Proclamation, which declared all slaves in seceded territories free. The move ensured no European power would fight to support the South since they had no wish to defend slavery.

Military strategies

The Art of War (1838) by Baron de Jomini was a popular textbook at the U.S. Military Academy at West Point. He defined military strategy and tactics as: "Strategy fixes the direction of movements, and we depend upon tactics for their execution." Henry L. Scott's *Military Dictionary* (1861) defined strategy as "the art of concerting a plan of campaign, combining a system of military operations determined by the end to be attained, the character of the enemy, the nature and resources of the country, and the means of attack and defense." Tactics was "the art of handling troops." Union generals realized that they would have to physically take Southern territory and fly their flag over it to win, while Confederate generals simply had to defend their territory. Given the new long-range, accurate rifled cannons and muskets, the clear tactical advantage lay with the defender in such a war.

Rifled

With spiral grooves on the inside of the barrel, which cause a projectile to spin and thus to fly more accurately.

Before the Civil War strategy, based on a European model, had three major strategic objectives: destroying the enemy's army in one decisive battle, seizing important sites, and capturing the enemy's capital city. A more effective Civil War strategy emerged—to fight a series of battles that individually might be indecisive, but that had a cumulative effect of allowing armies to protect or capture territory and wear down or drive off the enemy. Examples include Confederate General Robert E. Lee's success in driving off the Union army in the Seven Days' Battles and Union General Ulysses S. Grant's chasing Lee through Virginia in spring 1864.

Curriculum Context

It might be useful to be able to summarize the reason why the new strategy was more effective.

The Union increasingly used a strategy of making the Confederate economy and civilian population suffer. This involved blockading the Southern ports and also dividing east from west by taking the Mississippi River. If that could be achieved, vital foodstuffs could not go from west to east, nor war equipment from east to west. Union strategy also involved taking the South's industrial sites in Nashville, New Orleans, Atlanta, and Richmond. As a result of this strategy the main Union campaigns in the western theater were against New Orleans in 1862, Vicksburg and Baton Rouge in 1863,

Curriculum Context

The South had relatively few industrial centers, making the North's task easier.

The Raid as Strategy

Both sides used the raid on a grand scale to further their strategic ends. The two most famous large-scale raids were Confederate General Robert E. Lee's invasion of the north in 1863 and Union General William T. Sherman's invasion of Georgia in 1864 (the March to the Sea). In 1863 the Confederates' purpose was to keep Virginia's farmers safe to bring in that summer's crops, to reduce the pressure on the key Mississippi River points of Vicksburg and Baton Rouge, and to obtain much needed food for the Army of Northern Virginia. In 1864 the Union high command's purpose was to show Southern citizens that their forces were unable to protect them, and that Union forces could go wherever they wanted, whenever they wanted. Sherman's raid was meant to "illustrate the vulnerability of the South." Indeed, large-scale raids into Georgia, Alabama, and Virginia became the centerpiece of his 1864 strategy that eventually ended the war.

Atlanta and Savannah in 1864, and through the Carolinas in 1865. Throughout the war Richmond and the Shenandoah Valley were major targets in the eastern theater, as well as all the Southern ports.

Confederate strategy

After "cotton diplomacy" failed, the Confederates turned to a military strategy. Because its government was dependent on the goodwill of its citizens—the government being formed on the basis that each state was essentially its own nation—the Confederacy had to defend every inch of territory, whether it was essential to the overall war effort or not. Trading land to buy time as a strategy would have badly sapped Southern morale, as well as losing areas needed to grow food. The overall Confederate strategy was to garrison every threatened point, while concentrating forces at places that were specifically threatened by Union troops. It was simple to send a telegraph order to summon troops to threatened points, and railroads could get them to those points quickly and efficiently. The lack of an industrial base meant the Confederates could not maintain their telegraph lines and railroads, however, so communications became harder as time went on.

This strategy put the Confederacy at a disadvantage. The government had to garrison points that were not strategically important, while Union forces picked their targets and the sequence in which they attacked them. For example, Mobile, Alabama, had a large garrison that only saw action relatively late in the war. Other ports such as Savannah, Georgia, and Charleston, South Carolina, used huge resources that could have been used elsewhere much more effectively.

Public opinion and morale

Another element of Confederate strategy aimed to turn Northern public opinion against the war by causing heavy Union losses. It was thought that if the

Curriculum Context

What additional pressures did it bring to bear on the Confederacy that it was obliged to defend even nonessential territory?

Curriculum Context

Telegraphs and railroads were recent innovations that would change the shape of warfare for decades to come.

Lee's 1864 Strategy

Robert E. Lee wrote to Jefferson Davis on February 3, 1864, giving his ideas for Confederate strategy in the upcoming year: "If we could take the initiative and fall upon them unexpectedly we might derange their plans and embarrass them the whole summer. There are only two points east of the Mississippi where it now appears this could be done. If Longstreet could be strengthened or given greater mobility than he now possesses he might penetrate into Kentucky, where he could support himself, cut Grant's communications so as to compel him at least to detach from Johnston's front, and enable him to take the offensive and regain the ground we have lost. ... Longstreet can be given greater mobility by supplying him with horses and mules to mount his infantry. He can only be strengthened by detaching from Beauregard's, Johnston's, or this army. If I could draw Longstreet secretly and rapidly to me I might succeed in forcing Meade back to Washington, and exciting sufficient apprehension, at least for their own position, to weaken any movement against ours. All the cavalry would have to be left in Longstreet's present front and [General Samuel] Jones would have to be strengthened. ...

"We are not in a condition, and never have been, in my opinion, to invade the enemy's country with a prospect of permanent benefit. But we can alarm and embarrass him to some extent and thus prevent his undertaking anything of magnitude against us."

Confederacy could do this until the 1864 elections, a new Democratic president and a majority of Congress would recognize Southern independence. This goal led Lee to attack the Army of the Potomac repeatedly to destroy as much of it as possible. Raids into Northern territory, such as Braxton Bragg's into Kentucky in 1862 and Lee's into Pennsylvania in 1863, were designed to sap Northern civilian morale and raise support for Lincoln's political opponents. In the end, the Union capture of Atlanta, Georgia, turned Northerners against the Democrats, and Lincoln was reelected.

New battle tactics

Forces in the field soon learned to use different tactics. Frontal assaults by massed units did not work. The improved range and accuracy of rifled weapons taught the infantry to deploy in "open order," with soldiers advancing a few yards apart, taking advantage of cover

Curriculum Context

The surrender of Atlanta in September 1864, after a long siege, was a major boost for Northern morale that undermined the call by Lincoln's electoral opponent, George B. McClellan, for a truce with the Confederacy.

Curriculum Context

Students may be asked to describe the role of the North's superior industry in deciding the outcome of the war.

Shrapnel
Fragments of iron shells that have exploded.

where possible, rather than marching in massed ranks. Cavalry could no longer depend on winning a battle by charging with sabers drawn. Instead, they fought as dismounted skirmishers, with pistols and carbines.

Tactically, Northern industrial superiority was a major factor in the war. Union gunboats aided the army in battles such as Shiloh, Vicksburg, and Fort Donelson, and dominated Southern rivers. Union artillery was able to fire over the heads of infantry to provide support, while poorly made Southern fuses often exploded, sending shrapnel into friendly infantry.

Confederate innovation

The Confederates tried several tactics to compensate for superior Union numbers and resources. The armies of Tennessee and Northern Virginia formed shock battalions of sharpshooters who used open order skirmishing tactics rather than the shoulder-to-shoulder tactics called for in the manuals of the day.

The Confederate government allowed units of partisan rangers to operate behind enemy lines; this would force the North to garrison every outpost and damage morale. However, such rangers not only weakened regular Confederate forces by attracting men into their undisciplined ranks, but they also did very little harm to Union forces and were eventually largely disbanded.

A drawing by Alfred Waud of Union forces destroying a railroad bridge over the Chickahominy River in June 1862. The bridge was set on fire, then a train loaded with ammunition was sent across the bridge where it exploded, destroying train and bridge together. Cutting railroads was a key Civil War tactic.

Submarines

On February 17, 1864, the Union sloop USS *Housatonic* was attacked and sunk by the Confederate submarine CSS *Hunley* off Charleston Harbor. It was the first time that a warship had been successfully attacked by a submarine in wartime.

The Confederacy put a great deal of effort into developing submarines. Their first submarine, called the *Pioneer*, was constructed in New Orleans in early 1862 by a group led by Horace L. Hunley. The Union captured New Orleans before the *Pioneer* saw action.

Hunley and his group moved to Mobile, Alabama, where in 1863 they built an improved model named the *American Diver*, which sank during trials. A third version, bigger than the earlier models, was 40 ft (12 m) long and made of iron plates. Only 4 ft (1.2 m) wide and 3 ft (1 m) high, it barely gave the crew room to turn the hand crank that drove the propeller.

The new submarine was sent to help break the blockade at Charleston, but during sea trials it sank twice, killing Hunley himself. Charleston's commander, Pierre G.T. Beauregard, was persuaded to allow the submarine, now named the CSS *Hunley*, to put to sea again. This time it was armed with a sea mine attached to a 17-ft (5-m) spar protruding from its bow. The *Hunley* attacked the *Housatonic* on the surface, then submerged and disappeared along with its crew.

Union submarine experiments

The Union navy experimented with submarines, but with little success. In 1861 a Frenchman, Villeroi, built the *Alligator*, but it sank in a storm in 1863. The same year the American Submarine Company proposed building the *Intelligent Whale*, but failed to win government backing. The vessel was built after the war.

Curriculum Context

The development of the submarine is one of the few success stories of Confederate technological innovation during the war—although the *Hunley* sank soon after its victory over the *Housatonic*, killing all eight crew.

Union Army

At the start of the Civil War the U.S. Army consisted of 16,000 officers and men, most of them scattered in small military posts across the country. By the time the war ended, an estimated 2.5 million men had served in the Union army.

Curriculum Context

Should the president have the power to increase the size of the army? Some curricula include a critical analysis of the legality of such actions by Lincoln.

Quotas

Set minimum numbers of troops to be supplied by each state.

The U.S. government met the challenge of the Civil War by creating a large force of volunteers. The volunteer force, rather than the regular army, carried most of the burden of fighting. Recruitment for the Union army began on April 15, 1861, the day after Fort Sumter fell. President Lincoln called for 75,000 militia to serve for 90 days—the maximum time allowed by law. More than 91,000 men responded. The next month, without legal authority, Lincoln increased the regular army to 22,714 men and called for 42,000 volunteers to serve for three years. In July Congress retroactively approved both measures and called for 500,000 more volunteers. Most Union soldiers were infantrymen, but the North also raised 272 regiments of cavalry and numerous artillery units. The call-ups took the form of requests to Northern state governors for specific quotas of troops.

Recruiting volunteers

It was each governor's responsibility to find the quota of men. The task of recruitment was usually done at the local level, often by men prominent in the community, such as sheriffs, lawyers, and businessmen. They organized companies of 100 men and often went to war as their captain. The state governor assembled a group of 10 companies into a regiment, gave the regiment a name (for example, the 7th Illinois Volunteer Infantry) and a colonel, and presented it to the federal government. Only at that point was the regiment mustered into service. The system had its shortcomings. Although it maximized popular support, state governors often saw it as an opportunity for political patronage, so as regimental numbers diminished through battle casualties and disease, governors created new regiments rather than make good the losses. Wisconsin was the only state whose policy was to keep veteran units up to strength through a stream of replacements.

The training received by a Union regiment varied widely depending on the ability of its colonel and the time available before battle. Some regiments were led by professional officers, but many colonels had no more military experience than their men. They could be found reading military training manuals in their spare time.

Patronage

Handing out jobs or other benefits in return for political support.

Increasing the size of the army

Although the first wave of Union army volunteers nearly won the war in early 1862, a series of defeats in the summer of 1862 led to a call for 300,000 additional three-year volunteers, which actually produced 421,000 new troops. In March 1863 the U.S. Congress also passed a highly unpopular military conscription law. The law was resented: a man could be forced to serve against his will, while a wealthy man

Curriculum Context

McClellan was halted near Richmond in the Seven Days' Battles and defeated in the Second Battle of Bull Run.

Union Generals

No fewer than 583 men served as generals in the Union army. Of them, only 217 were graduates of the U.S. Military Academy at West Point, but many more had previous military experience. A number were so-called "political generals," appointed primarily in order to maximize political support for the Union war effort. Some political generals, like John Logan, became excellent combat commanders, but many, such as Nathaniel P. Banks, were notoriously poor battlefield leaders.

Outgeneraled by Confederate General Thomas "Stonewall" Jackson in the Shenandoah Valley campaign of 1862, Banks abandoned so many supplies to Jackson that Confederates called him "Commissary Banks." Often these political generals were better suited to administrative roles and so were chosen to govern civilians in Union-occupied areas. Benjamin F. Butler and Banks, for example, were two political generals called on by Lincoln to serve as military governors in Louisiana.

Curriculum Context

Many curricula ask students to analyze the complex causes of the draft riots in the North.

could pay a $300 fee to be excused from a call-up, and he could be excused army service altogether if he hired a substitute. Most people could not afford this and riots took place when some Northerners resisted the draft.

The draft was also inefficient. Only 52,000 men were actually drafted. Another 118,000 substitutes were enlisted. Fewer than seven out of every 100 men who served in the Union army entered as a result of the draft. Since the draft was used only in areas where volunteering was inadequate, it encouraged Northern communities to get as many men as possible to enlist voluntarily.

Black regiments

African Americans were another source of manpower for the Union. Initially barred from military service, by mid-1862 blacks had begun to serve on a limited and unofficial basis. Full-scale recruitment began following Lincoln's Emancipation Proclamation, which came into force on January 1, 1863. An estimated 186,000 African Americans eventually served in the Union army, most of them former slaves. By the end of the war one Union soldier in ten was black. Almost 100,000 white men from Confederate states also joined the Union army: Their states had seceded, but they remained loyal to the Union. Union territory was divided into a number of geographical military departments, each headed by

Part of the 6th Maine Infantry on parade after the Battle of Fredericksburg. As a rule, the Union army did not replenish existing units; instead, it raised new ones.

Motivation to Fight

What motivated Union soldiers to enlist? Historians still debate the extent to which soldiers on both sides understood the political stakes involved. Some were clear about their reasons for joining up: Quincy Campbell wrote of his decision to join the Fifth Iowa in July 1861: "I have volunteered to fight in this war for the Union and a government. I have left the peaceful walks of life and buckled on the harness of war not from any feeling of enthusiasm, nor incited by any hopes of honor [or] glory, but because I believe that duty to my country and my God bid me assist in crushing this wicked rebellion against our government, which men have instigated to secure their own promotion … and to secure the extension of that blighting curse—slavery—o'er our fair land."

Although Campbell was among relatively few Union soldiers with strong antislavery convictions from the start of the war, by mid-1862 many men had seen at firsthand the way in which slavery aided the Confederate war effort. Increasingly they agreed with a Union colonel who wrote in September 1862: "Crippling the institution of slavery is … striking a blow at the heart of the rebellion." African American soldiers were fighting against slavery and to secure the same legal and political rights as their white counterparts.

a major general and usually named for a river, such as the Department of the Potomac, which covered much of Virginia and its field army, the Army of the Potomac.

Generals-in-chief

At the head of the Union army was a single general-in-chief. At the start of the war the post was held by Winfield Scott (April–November 1861), then George B. McClellan (November 1861–March 1862), Henry W. Halleck (July 1862–March 1864), and finally Ulysses S. Grant (March 1864–May 1865). Only Grant exercised strong, direct military leadership; the others saw the job as mainly administrative in nature. The Union army also had very able men in charge of supply and transportation. Chief among them were Montgomery C. Meigs, the quartermaster general, and David C. McCullum, superintendent of Union military railroads. Their effective organization of equipping, supplying, and transporting the Union armies over vast distances, contributed greatly to the Union victory.

Curriculum Context

You may be asked to name individuals who had a decisive influence on the course of the war.

Union Navy

At the outbreak of the Civil War the Union had a very limited number of ships. It was in a better position than the South, but not by much. Lincoln's appointment of Gideon Welles as secretary of the navy did much to improve the situation.

President Lincoln appointed Gideon Welles Secretary of the Navy in 1860. Welles was ably supported by Assistant Secretary of the Navy Gustavus V. Fox, a naval officer whose efficiency and knowledge helped in the urgent task of building up the Union navy. At the outbreak of war the Union navy had 90 ships, of which only 41 were serviceable. Personnel included about 1,500 officers—around 300 resigned to join the Confederacy—and 7,500 enlisted men. Lincoln's 1861 proclamation of a blockade of Southern ports meant the navy had to enlarge rapidly, since such a proclamation was only valid under international law if foreign vessels were physically stopped from entering or leaving a blockaded port.

Blockade

To use naval vessels and other defenses to prevent cargos reaching another country.

Increasing the fleet

Union navy officials immediately began commissioning new vessels. They bought civilian vessels to fit out for wartime use, including double-ended ferry boats that proved valuable in river warfare. The vessels were equipped with armor and guns, and sent to duty stations along the coasts and rivers. By the end of 1861 the Union navy had nearly 200 vessels in service and 22,000 naval personnel. This number grew until by the end of the war the navy had some 670 ships and 51,500 men.

Curriculum Context

Uniquely, the navies of the Civil War were more concerned with river warfare than with coastal or ocean operations.

Naval squadrons

In May 1861 the navy organized two blockading squadrons, one for the Atlantic coast and one for the Gulf of Mexico. The two were later divided into four:

the North and South Atlantic Blockading Squadrons and the East and West Gulf Blockading Squadrons. These squadrons, each commanded by a commodore (a temporary flag officer position until the rank of rear admiral was created in July 1862), handled all blockading duties.

The opening of the Mississippi River was a major goal for the Union navy, and the Mississippi Squadron was also created in May 1861. It later included regular naval vessels and the new ironclads (steam-driven armored gunboats) as well. An ironclad-building program on the upper reaches of the Mississippi very rapidly produced the gunboats for this squadron.

Squadrons along the Atlantic coast also maintained ironclads on the many rivers that opened to the sea. Ironclads were used in a number of joint army/navy operations. The Potomac Flotilla was organized to keep the Potomac clear and to defend Washington, D.C., the Union capital. There were several overseas squadrons. Squadrons off South America, Europe, and Africa had the duty of destroying Confederate commerce raiders, which preyed on Union merchant ships.

Naval officers

Naval officers were divided into two types. Executive officers were in charge of vessels. From August 1863 they wore a star over their gold sleeve rank stripes. The

A naval gun crew drills with a 9-inch (22-cm) Dahlgren gun, the standard cannon of the U.S. Navy at the outbreak of war. Crews drilled with guns on a daily basis. The netting was to prevent the enemy boarding the vessel.

Curriculum Context

The ironclad-building program is a good example of the North's industrial superiority.

second type of officers were specialists. They included surgeons; naval constructors; paymasters, who handled ships' supplies and pay; engineers, who had to maintain onboard machinery, an important task as technology developed; chaplains, who were responsible for the spiritual life of sailors; and math and chemistry professors, who taught midshipmen and cadets chemistry, geometry, and calculus. The specialized officers, who did not wear the executive star, held "relative rank" with executive officers. For example, a fleet surgeon was ranked equal to a captain, although he only commanded individuals in his field.

The traditional training of professional naval officers was through years of sea service. However, to produce the officers needed for a rapidly enlarging navy, senior midshipmen were commissioned immediately in 1861, before their schooling was finished. This did not make up the shortage of officers, so on July 24, 1861, the secretary of the navy was authorized to appoint acting, volunteer officers below the rank or relative rank of lieutenant. The volunteer officers came mostly from the U.S. merchant marine, which had been greatly reduced by the successful attacks of Confederate commerce raiders. They had to pass an exam before receiving their appointments and were then trained in gunnery and seamanship in schools based in various navy yards. At its peak the Union navy had 7,500 volunteer officers.

Recruitment

The navy was at a disadvantage in recruiting because state army units offered volunteers bounties to enlist. Like the officers, most volunteer enlisted men came from the merchant marine. They joined because they were familiar with shipboard life. Senior enlisted personnel were petty and chief petty officers with specialized jobs and were appointed by each ship's captain. In all, 84,500 men enlisted in the Union navy during the war.

Black sailors had worked on naval vessels for years and were accepted into the unsegregated Union navy from the beginning of the war. They made up between 8 and 25 percent of all Union navy personnel and there were many acts of naval daring by black sailors such as Robert Smalls, a slave on the Confederate transport steamer, the CSS *Planter*. On May 13, 1862, Smalls sailed the *Planter* out of Charleston Harbor with the help of 12 other slaves while the ship's white officers were asleep onshore. Once past the Confederate guns, he handed over the ship to the Union navy. As a result of this heroic action, Smalls was feted in the North. He later served with distinction in the Union navy.

Curriculum Context

The navy was unsegregated at a time when the Union army was still segregated.

Training

New volunteers were first sent aboard receiving ships. They were old ships that had been converted into floating barracks and training facilities. Here they received their uniforms, which they had to pay for, and were given basic training in seamanship and gunnery. Sailors were sent from the receiving ships to their duty stations as soon as they were needed, regardless of how much training they had had. In fact, training was fairly rare; most new sailors learned their jobs once they reached their duty stations.

Curriculum Context

Smalls' story is relatively little known, so it could be used when discussing individuals whose actions impacted the course of the war.

The Union gunboat USS *Commodore Perry* and its crew on the Pamunkey River in Virginia in 1864. The vessel was originally a ferryboat but was converted into a gunboat to boost the number of ships in the Union navy.

Weapons and Firearms

A huge variety of weapons and ammunition were used during the Civil War. Weapons were undergoing a period of rapid development, and the improvements revolutionized the way that battles were fought.

Curriculum Context

Throughout the war, the weapons available shaped the way in which troops were trained and battles were fought.

Ramrod

A long, thin metal rod kept in brackets beneath the rifle barrel.

The most widely used firearm was the infantryman's rifle musket. A single-shot weapon, loaded down the muzzle with a ramrod, it was fired using a small copper percussion cap that fitted over the breech. One cap was needed per round. The cartridges were made of paper, often tied with twine, that contained the lead bullet or ball at one end and the charge of black powder at the other. An infantryman could carry 40 rounds in a cartridge box on his belt, plus as many as he could carry in his pockets. The percussion caps, about a quarter-inch (50 mm) in diameter, were kept separately in a small leather pouch, suspended from the soldier's belt.

Loading ready to fire

To load and fire the rifle musket, the infantrymen had to learn a drill of up to a dozen commands and 20 separate movements that quickly and efficiently maneuvered rifle, ramrod, cartridge, and percussion cap together. At the command "Load" the soldier would bring the musket down from his shoulder and hold it upright, while his right hand went to the cartridge box. "Handle cartridge" brought the cartridge out of the box to the soldier's mouth. He would then tear off the end with the gunpowder in, pour the powder and ball down the rifle muzzle, and push the cartridge paper down after it. "Draw rammer" would have the ramrod out of its place under the barrel, and with the order "Ram" it would be rammed down the muzzle, pushing powder, ball, and paper snugly into the breech. The ramrod was then returned to its place.

Firing the rifle musket

With the next command, "Prime," the soldier brought the musket up, pulled the hammer back to halfcock, pulled off the used percussion cap, and fitted a new one from the pouch at his belt. At "Ready" the right hand would go to the lock, the weapon would be brought up vertically, and the hammer drawn back to full cock. On "Aim" the soldier brought the musket down into his right shoulder and sighted over the muzzle, while his finger found the trigger. Then the order came to "Fire."

In combat an infantryman loaded and fired his gun almost without thinking, although there were some mistakes. Ramrods were left in muzzles and shot out with the bullet, while some men forgot to replace the percussion cap after every round or reloaded without realizing their weapon had not fired. After the Battle of Gettysburg as many as 18,000 discarded muskets were found with more than one round in them.

Curriculum Context

The idea behind constant training drill was to make the actions of firing a gun second nature to soldiers.

Change in tactics

The parade-ground drill became obsolete later on. Because of the intensity of gunfire, troops found it impossible to carry out their drill without taking high casualties. Instead, infantry advanced in loose formation in short runs, firing and then kneeling or lying down to avoid enemy fire and then reloading.

The Springfield Rifle

One of the most widely issued rifles was the U.S. Model 1861 Springfield, of which over a million were produced, most of them at the Union Arsenal at Springfield, Massachusetts. They were issued to the Union army, but the Confederates got hold of huge numbers of them after some of the Union's defeats. During July and August 1862 General Robert E. Lee's Army of Northern Virginia collected 55,000 new rifles after beating the Army of the Potomac during the Seven Days' Battles and the Second Battle of Bull Run, as Union soldiers threw away their weapons in retreat.

Repeating Rifles

From 1864 the single-shot rifle musket was becoming increasingly obsolete. The Union army began to be issued with new rifles such as the Sharps and the Spencer, which were breechloaders that could fire six to eight rounds before they needed to be reloaded.

The Spencer cartridge was made up of a copper case containing a lead bullet and powder charge with its own primer. This made it more reliable than other ignition systems, such as those requiring primer caps or tapes. The Confederates could not match this firepower. Even if they salvaged abandoned breechloading rifles from the battlefield, they did not have the industrial resources in the South to manufacture the new kind of metal cartridges they fired. As one Union soldier wrote of his new repeating rifle, "I think the Johnny [Rebs] are getting rattled. ... They say we are not fair, that we have guns that we load up on Sunday and shoot all the rest of the week."

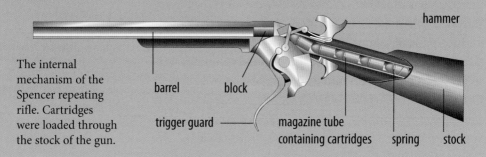

The internal mechanism of the Spencer repeating rifle. Cartridges were loaded through the stock of the gun.

barrel   block   hammer

trigger guard

magazine tube containing cartridges   spring   stock

The technical innovation that made the rifle musket so deadly was its rifling, the spiral groove cut into the inside of the barrel that spun the bullet, increasing its range and accuracy. A Frenchman, Captain Minié, developed a conical lead bullet with a hollow base in the 1840s. When the rifle was fired, the gases of the exploding black powder pushed out the sides of the bullet to grip the rifling in the barrel. The Minié bullet was widely used in the war. A rifle musket firing such a bullet could kill with accuracy up to 500 yards (450 m), while at 1,000 yards (900 m) the Minié bullet could still penetrate 4 inches (10 cm) of wood.

Both sides imported rifles from Europe, especially at the start of the war, when there were not enough weapons for the thousands of volunteers. Some

Black powder

An mixture of potassium nitrate or sodium nitrate, charcoal, and sulfur used as the explosive in Civil War ammunition.

imports such as the Model 1853 Enfield from Britain, of which both sides bought more than 400,000 each, performed better than others. Belgian rifles had the worst reputation.

Shortage of weapons

The shortage of firearms was particularly acute in the Confederacy. At the start of the war the Confederacy had only about 150,000 rifle muskets, most taken from Union arsenals. By the First Battle of Bull Run (July 1861) they had all been given out, and new volunteers were asked to bring their own weapons. Some states issued pleas to civilians to donate firearms, while others took stronger measures—Tennessee passed a law allowing firearms to be seized from private homes. The shortage of weapons was so bad in spring 1862 that General "Stonewall" Jackson proposed companies of men be armed with pikes—long, steel-tipped spears.

Soldiers on both sides seemed to favor obsolete weaponry. Confederate soldiers carried big fighting knives, known as "Bowie knives," with blades up to 19 inches (48 cm) long in 1861; they rarely survived into the second year of war. One Union cavalry regiment was armed with lances, which proved useless when they faced Confederate cavalry in 1862. Mown down by gunfire, the Union troops fled in disorder.

Bayonets and sabers

Knives and lances were symbols of military prowess, like the bayonet and the cavalry saber. Every rifle musket was issued with a bayonet, usually about 18 inches (45 cm) long, with spike-shaped triangular blades. Bayonets were meant to instill fear in an enemy when used by a mass of charging infantry, but the range and power of the rifle musket made such charges suicidal. Bayonets played a less important part in combat as the war went on, and the cavalry saber was gradually replaced by the revolver and carbine.

Arsenals

Official stores of weapons and ammunition for military use.

Bowie knife

The Bowie (boo-ee) knife was named for the famed early 19th-century frontiersman Jim Bowie.

Curriculum Context

The abandonment of bladed weapons is an example of the impact of technology on the nature of the fighting.

Zouaves

Among the ranks of soldiers clad in standard blue, gray, and butternut brown uniforms, men wearing more colorful uniforms fought in the Civil War. They were Zouave infantry units, which were fielded by both Union and Confederacy.

The Zouave (pronounced "zwahve") regiments owed their appearance to the dress of North African tribesmen. The uniform consisted of a short, collarless jacket over a sleeveless vest, a long waist sash, short baggy pants, leather leggings or greaves, and white gaiters. Headwear was a fez, a kind of skullcap with a tassel. The men of one Union regiment, the 146th New York, even wore turbans. The colors were also unusual, being a combination of light blue and red with a lot of decoration, especially on the jacket, which often featured ornate ribbon patterns and rows of buttons.

Curriculum Context

Like many other aspects of American culture, military thinking at the start of the war was dominated by European influences.

French fashion

The Zouaves were a French innovation and owed their origins to a tribe in Algeria known as the Zou Oua, who helped France conquer and colonize that country in the 1830s. Their courage and fighting skills were so impressive the French Army adopted their tactics and style of dress, and formed their own regiments, which they named Zouaves.

Crimean War

A war fought on the Black Sea between the Russian Empire on one side and an alliance of France, Britain, the Ottoman Empire, and their allies on the other.

Their influence in the United States began when U.S. Army officers returned home from the Crimean War (1853–1856), having acted as official observers to the French Army. George B. McClellan, who later became general-in-chief of the Union army described the Zouaves as the ideal of what a soldier should be. After an endorsement like that, it did not take long for militia companies across the United States to begin adopting the Zouave uniform and copying their extravagant style of drill.

Elmer E. Ellsworth, from New York State, in 1857 formed the United States Zouave Cadets in Chicago. Ellsworth trained his men and proclaimed them the best drilled and most disciplined militia company in the Midwest. In 1860 he took 50 of his Zouaves on a tour of a dozen states, giving public displays of drill that drew crowds of thousands. At the start of war in April 1861 Ellsworth traveled to New York to raise a regiment of Zouaves and called on Manhattan's firefighters to volunteer. These men, who were already used to teamwork, discipline, and physical danger, answered his call; and by April 29 the 11th New York Infantry, known as "Ellsworth's Fire Zouaves," paraded down Broadway. Companies of firefighters in other cities became eager to wear the fez of the Zouaves, and several other "Fire Zouaves" sprung up, including "Baxter's Philadelphia Fire Zouaves," officially the 72nd Pennsylvania Infantry.

Ellsworth's Fire Zouaves fought at the First Battle of Bull Run on July 21, 1861. By the Battle of Antietam on September 17, 1862, the Army of the Potomac fielded three Zouave regiments: the 9th New York, "Hawkin's Zouaves"; the 5th New York, "Duryea's Zouaves"; and the 114th Pennsylvania, "Collis's Zouaves."

Southern Zouaves

Confederate Zouaves tended to come from Louisiana, where French influence was strong. In the early years of the war the South could boast of the "Louisiana Tiger Zouaves," "Wheat's Tigers" from New Orleans, and "Coppen's Louisiana Zouaves." There were also Confederate Zouave units from Virginia and Maryland.

Zouaves were expensive to maintain, and their conspicuous dress made them targets in battle. While the Union army could still afford to muster new regiments as late as 1864, by 1863 Confederate Zouaves existed in name only, their exotic uniforms worn out and their extravagant drill out of place.

Curriculum Context

Accurate long-range weapons made it dangerous to wear bright colors on the battlefield as the war went on.

Glossary

absenteeism Being absent from duty without permission.

amnesty A pardon granted by a government.

arsenals Official stores of weapons and ammunition for military use.

battery An artillery unit, consisting of a number of guns and their crews.

black powder A mixture of potassium nitrate or sodium nitrate, charcoal, and sulfur used as the explosive in Civil War ammunition.

blockade To use naval vessels and other defenses to prevent cargos reaching another country.

blockade-runner A sailor or ship that ran through the Union blockade of Southern ports during the Civil War.

bounty A one-off payment made to encourage men to enlist in the army.

Bowie knife The Bowie (boo-ee) knife was named for the famed early 19th-century frontiersman Jim Bowie.

breechloader A rifle that is loaded through a chamber in the barrel, not from the end of the barrel.

brigade A military unit of around 5,000 soldiers made up of between two and six regiments. The brigade was the common tactical unit of the Civil War.

caliber The diameter of a bullet or other projectile.

carbine A light, short-barreled, repeating firearm designed to be used by cavalry.

cavalry Mounted soldiers; the role of cavalry changed considerably during the course of the war.

commerce raiding The capture of Union merchant vessels at sea to disrupt the North's ability to trade.

company A military unit consisting of 50 to 100 men commanded by a captain. There were 10 companies in a regiment. Companies were raised by individual states.

conscripts People who are forced to join an army without any individual choice.

contact fuse A fuse that detonated explosives when it was impacted by a hard surface, such as the hull of a ship.

corduroy roads Log roads, named for their resemblance to the ridges on corduroy fabric.

corps The largest military unit in the Civil War armies, consisting of two or more divisions. Corps were established in the Union army in March 1862 and in the Confederate army in November 1862.

counterattack To attack the enemy after it has attacked you

court martial A military court.

diplomacy The practice of maintaining relations between countries.

division The second largest military unit in the Civil War armies. A division was made up of three or four brigades and was commanded by a brigadier or major general. There were between two and four divisions in a corps.

entrenchments Defensive trenches dug into the ground, often protected by earthworks.

flintlock A firearm fired by a spark struck by a flint when the trigger is pulled.

forage Food for animals.

garrison A unit of soldiers based in a stronghold in order to defend a particular town or area.

infantry Foot soldiers.

ironclad A ship protected by iron armor.

lance A long, metal-tipped spear carried by cavalrymen.

Medal of Honor The Medal of Honor for gallantry in action was created by President Lincoln in 1863.

merchant ship A vessel that is used to transport trade goods or passengers, as opposed to a warship.

militias Local forces of civilian volunteers who could perform military duties in time of emergency.

mine Known during the Civil War as "torpedoes," mines are explosive devices, usually concealed, designed to destroy enemy soldiers and transportation.

mortar A type of short-barreled cannon that threw shells in a high arc over enemy fortifications, commonly used in siege warfare.

muzzleloaded Muzzleloaded weapons were loaded through the end of the barrel.

mutiny An organized or large-scale revolt against military orders.

NCO Non-commissioned officer: a junior officer who has been promoted from the ranks of the army.

partisans Guerrilla fighters operating behind enemy lines.

patronage Handing out jobs or other benefits in return for political support.

ramrod A long, thin metal rod kept in brackets beneath the rifle barrel.

recoil The kickback of a gun or cannon as it is fired.

reconnaissance Something done for the purpose of gathering information about the enemy, their position, and plans.

regiment A military unit consisting of 10 companies of 100 men at full strength. In practice, most Civil War regiments were much smaller than this. Raised by state governors, they were usually composed of men from the same area. The Civil War soldier's main loyalty and sense of identity was connected to his regiment.

rifling A technique used on both guns and cannons that allowed weapons to fire further and with greater accuracy than previously. Rifled barrels had spiral grooves cut into the inside, which gave a bullet or shell spin when fired.

saber A heavy sword with one sharp edge and a slightly curved blade.

sabotage To destroy key property or otherwise interfere with an enemy's ability to operate.

seeing the elephant Experiencing frontline action; the phrase was common in the United States in the mid-19th century, meaning to experience a great emotion.

scurvy A disease caused by a lack of Vitamin C.

sharpshooter A marksman whose task was to pick off individual enemy soldiers, often at distance, using highly accurate rifle fire.

shot Small spherical pellets that are packed into canisters or shells.

shrapnel Fragments of iron shells that have exploded.

siege To surround and cut off supplies to an army or town to force surrender.

small arms Weapons that are carried and fired by hand.

smoothbore Without rifled grooves on the inside of the barrel.

snipers Expert marksmen whose task was to target and kill individuals on the enemy side.

spar A long, rounded spear projecting from something.

subordination The state of being junior to someone else.

transports Ships for carrying military equipment or supplies.

Further Research

BOOKS

Adler, Dennis. *Guns of the Civil War*. Zenith Press, 2001.

Alexander, Bevin. *Lost Victories: The Military Genius of Stonewall Jackson*. Hippocrene Books, 2004.

Alexander, Bevin. *How the South Could Have Won the Civil War: The Fatal Errors that Led to Confederate Defeat*. Three Rivers Press, 2008.

Barney, William L. *The Oxford Encyclopedia of the Civil War*. Oxford University Press, 2011.

Bearss, Edwin C. and J. Parker Hills. *Receding Tide: Vicksburg and Gettysburg—The Campaigns that Changed the Civil War*. National Geographic, 2010.

Bilby, Joseph G. *Civil War Firearms: Their Historical Background and Tactical Use*. Da Capo Press, 2005.

Catton, Bruce. *The Civil War*. Boston, MA: Houghton Mifflin, 1987.

Civil War Preservation Trust. *Civil War Sites: The Official Guide to the Civil War Discovery Trail*. Globe Pequot, 2007.

Coles, David J., et al. *Encyclopedia of the American Civil War: Political, Social, and Military History*. W.W. Norton and Company, 2002.

Engle, Stephen D. *The American Civil War: The War in the West 1861–July 1863*. London: Fitzroy Dearborn, 2001.

Gallagher, Gary W. *The American Civil War: The War in the East 1861–May 1863*. London: Fitzroy Dearborn, 2001.

Gallagher, Gary W., and Robert Krick. *The American Civil War: The War in the East 1863–1865*. London: Fitzroy Dearborn, 2001.

Glatthaar, Joseph T. *The American Civil War: The War in the West 1863–1865*. London: Fitzroy Dearborn, 2001.

Grant, Ulysses S. *Personal Memoirs*. New York: Crescent Books, 1995.

Hendrickson, Robert. *The Road to Appomattox*. New York: John Wiley, 1998.

Holzer, Harold, and Craig Symonds. *The New York Times Complete Civil War 1861–1865*. Black Dog and Leventhal Publishers, 2010.

Marrin, Albert. *Commander in Chief: Abraham Lincoln in the Civil War*. New York: Dutton, 1997.

Mosier, John. *Grant: Lessons in Leadership*. Palgrave Macmillan, 2006.

Plaster, John L. *Sharpshooting in the Civil War*. Paladin Press, 2009.

Robertson, James I. *Soldiers Blue and Gray*. Columbia, SC: University of South Carolina Press, 1998.

Schindler, Stanley (editor). *Memoirs of Robert E. Lee*. New York: Crescent Books, 1994.

Smith, Gene. *Lee and Grant: A Dual Biography*. New York: McGraw-Hill, 1984.

Stoker, Donald. *The Grand Design: Strategy and the U.S. Civil War*. Oxford University Press, 2010.

Tucker, Spencer C. (ed.). *The Civil War Naval Encyclopedia* (2 volumes). ABC–Clio, 2010.

Trudeau, Noah Andre. *Robert E, Lee: Lessons in Leadership*. Palgrave Macmillan, 2010.

Walsh, George. *Those Damn Horse Soldiers: True Tales of the Civil War Cavalry*. Forge Books, 2006.

Woodworth, Steven E. *Sherman: Lessons in Leadership*. Palgrave Macmillan, 2010.

INTERNET RESOURCES

These general sites have comprehensive links to a large number of Civil War topics:

http://sunsite.utk.edu/civil-war/warweb.html

http://civilwarhome.com/

http://americancivilwar.com/

http://www.civil-war.net/

http://www2.cr.nps.gov/abpp/battles/bystate.htm
This part of the National Parks Service site allows you to search for battles by state

http://pdmusic.org/civilwar.html
Sound files and words to Civil War songs

http://www.civilwarmed.org/
National Museum of Civil War Medicine

http://memory.loc.gov/ammem/aaohtml/exhibit/aopart4.html
Civil War section of the African American Odyssey online exhibition at the Library of Congress

http://valley.vcdh.virginia.edu/
The Valley of the Shadow Project: details of Civil War life in two communities, one Northern and one Southern

http://www.civilwarhome.com/records.htm
Battle reports by commanding generals from the Official Records

http://www.cwc.lsu.edu/
The United States Civil War Center at Lousiana State University

http://www.nps.gov/gett/gettkidz/soldslang.htm
Civil War slang from the site of the Gettysburg National Military Park

http://www.sonofthesouth.net/leefoundation/ebooks.htm
The Robert E. Lee Foundation digital library of books about Lee and about the Civil War generally

Index

Page numbers in *italic* refer to illustrations and captions.